BREAKING THE RULES

BREAKING THE RULES

HOME STYLE FOR THE WAY WE LIVE TODAY

CHRISTY FERER

WITH RISA PALAZZO

PRINCIPAL PHOTOGRAPHY BY JEAN-FRANÇOIS JAUSSAUD AND JOSHUA MCHUGH

SIMON & SCHUSTER

NEW YORK   LONDON   TORONTO   SYDNEY   SINGAPORE

Preface

Never use big furniture in small rooms.

Stick to one style, one color thread, and one period throughout your home.

Pink is only for bedrooms and bathrooms.

Sleek surfaces and black accents work best in contemporary environments.

Living rooms are formal showcases for guests.

Wrought iron and stone belong in the garden.

These age-old rules are *over*. Personalization reigns. These days we are taking control of our living spaces and molding them to our every need, mood, and last-minute flea-market find. Whose house is it, anyway? Yours, *remember*? That old adage "rules were made to be broken" is tremendously liberating. Now we are actually *living* in the living room—eating, working, and watching television in a space that was for years almost off-limits as anything but a showplace. These days the dining room is not just for eating but can be used as an office or perhaps a playroom. I even have a very sophisticated friend who transforms her Louis-the-Something bathroom, garnished with gold-plate fixtures, into a dining room for dinner parties. I love the idea of all her aristocratic chums dining in her bathroom, seated on top of a tub she has transformed into a banquette.

Styling one's home is still about wanting to live with beautiful things in an environment you can't wait to come back to . . . but the emphasis is on comfort, not conformity. More and more the ornamental has to have some practicality—the statue in the front hall may end up with a hat tossed on its head. Unexpected ideas such as using a crystal chandelier in a log cabin or felt squares as flooring boast an individuality that is applauded. No more obsessing over coordinating colors and fabrics. The new chic doesn't entail rooms that are "done" but rather those that reflect your tastes, passions, and idiosyncrasies. It is a style of decorating that is so close to the heart, it is timeless.

Breaking the rules allows you to start a revolution in your own home, and it gives you the courage to go ahead and let those style "security blankets" unravel. Show off your most beloved accessories in new ways, experiment with your furniture to create new spaces, find fresh ways of living from room to room. In showing how others have played with lighting, screens, and color or mixed old with new, expensive with inexpensive, this book is meant to inspire and get you to try something new.

Take the plunge: put an oversize, cushy couch in a tiny room, try a funky fifties vase on a Louis XIV–style desk, upholster your best piece of furniture with a Navajo blanket, paint your dining room red, put your costume jewelry in a beautiful bowl as an accessory. Today, this individuality is all not only allowed but celebrated.

Playing it safe with your home is such a BORE. It's like being a painter and leaving a canvas blank. Throwing out the rule book will remove the fear of making mistakes and give you the license to design a room that embraces you with the warmth of personal creativity the minute you walk in.

Once you see how others have mixed and not matched, or decorated a man's study in blushing pink, or used a shell as a faucet or an entry foyer as an office, I hope surfaces, objects, and spaces will never quite seem the same.

What *Breaking the Rules* offers is my small window on the world, the style snapshots that have affected my eye and the way I have played with my home. I am blessed because I have been exposed to so many people who have pushed the envelope and broken more than a convention or two. Now I am sharing that with you.

So turn the page, get ready to break a few rules, and go wild.

—CHRISTY FERER

COL OR

Color Commitment

Shelves have been painted to blend with the wall and the china. Even sponges play along with the color scheme.

Forget color wheels and other academic approaches to choosing what colors go with what. Color has more to do with emotion than with technicalities. Think about what color does. It pulls you in, or pushes you away. It can easily shock. Or calm.

There is no reason to follow anybody else's idea of what colors you should use in your home. If you aren't sure, just look through your clothes closet. One or two colors will repeat over and over. Trust yourself. If you love a color, use it. Let your eye and your instinct lead you to the colors you love to live with.

Today, color therapists use the energy of certain colors to affect mind and body. Pediatric wards are often painted bubble-gum pink to soothe children. Before going on stage, performers wait in a "green room," where the relaxing qualities of the color help calm performance jitters. Blue, known to lower blood pressure, respiration, and heart rate, is ideal for a meditative space. The yellow legal pad was born from the belief that yellow stimulates the intellect and the memory. Red, the first color a newborn reacts to, stimulates the appetite, making it the color of choice in restaurants.

The human eye recognizes at least ten million colors. Don't feel bad if you can't decide what colors to paint your bathroom. Take your time, you'll find them.

Color Cooks
In Bette Midler's kitchen, Crayola-colored handles give a color jolt to a sleek stove. "I love color," she says. "I don't care where it comes from . . . walls, flowers, anything. Color is a subliminal source of joy and happiness that sets off something that lifts your spirits."

Neutral Black
Donna Karan combines silver and black in her kitchen, which neutralizes the tone of the room and maintains the thread of black that unifies the apartment.

"Stick to neutrals. They go with anything."

This rule is responsible for decades of boring rooms. People think neutral means only beige, white, or black. True, these colors blend easily with other colors and are easy to live with, but so are lots of other more interesting colors. When toned down with white or black, green coordinates with almost all colors, making it nature's neutral. Celadon, olive, khaki and steel gray are the "new" neutrals, easily pulling together complex color palettes.

Remember what the legendary Vogue editor Diana Vreeland said: "Shocking pink is the navy blue of India." The point is that what is neutral for one culture or person is radical for another. Remember this too: Almost any color becomes a neutral when it stands on its own and isn't made to coordinate with another color.

"White and bright colors show dirt. Keep away from them."

This might have been true at one time, but not anymore. Today's fabrics are usually washable, making most colors right for most rooms. Ditto for paints. Being practical doesn't mean being drab. A white bedroom is an oasis at the end of a busy day: White drapes, rug, furniture, and linens turn chaos to calm.

"Bedrooms should be done in soothing colors like blue to help you sleep."

Today, bedrooms are used for many things besides sleeping. People snack, read, watch TV, catch up on paper-work, make phone calls, meditate, and exercise in them. They are thoroughly utilized throughout the day as well as over-night and should be decorated in your favorite color. If it's orange, go for it.

Really Red
The subtle pattern of this old silk damask softens and gives texture to the intense red, while the crystal sconce provides a glowing yellow contrast.

Rub It In
A formal space is made comfortable with casual colors. The wall molding is exaggerated by rubbing on a deeper tone of the wall color.

"Pink is a feminine color, best used for private spaces like bathrooms or bedrooms."

Pink is unisex. You don't have to wear lipstick to appreciate the rosy glow this color gives your complexion and your outlook on life. Yes, pink is for bathrooms. But it is also for living rooms, entryways, dining rooms, and any other room of the house you want to use it in. My husband's study is painted pink. French designer Philippe Model uses pink throughout his apartment. For him, it "works on the unconscious and makes us feel at ease."

"Pipes, fuse boxes, outlets, water heaters, etc. are ugly and should be painted to blend in."

Many contemporary architects actually choose to celebrate the beams and bolts that hold a house together and deliberately draw the eye to them. Instead of trying to camouflage them, highlight them with color to make them part of the decoration.

"Primary colors are for children's rooms."

The natural world is infused with primary colors—in a bright blue sky, a vivid yellow sunflower, or a shiny red apple. These colors can look wonderful and very sophisticated in our homes, too. For those who object to the brightness of primary colors, consider using a lighter shade.

There is nothing like red to cozy up a space, because it advances rather than recedes, but it will still have the same effect if it is made less intense by watering it down into a wash or softening it to rosy pink. Even a pale yellow brings sunshine into a dark room. Blue expands space and gives the feeling of fresh air to cramped quarters.

Primary colors can also work their magic if they are used as accents rather than in broad strokes. A strong red door frame can add a vivid thrill to a room that might not be able to handle a red wall.

"There should be at least three colors in a room."

The impetus behind this long-standing rule can be summed up in one word—variety. The fear is that using any fewer than three colors will result in a bland room. The problem with this rule lies in its assumption that one color equals one shade. Colors consist of many shades.

If you've ever tried to match a pair of white shoes to a white handbag *perfectly* you'll know what I mean. It's not easy, but if you can create a room using just one shade of one color or a "non-color" like black you will make a strong statement. You can also exploit the rich range of shades within a single color to design a space with tremendous variety. Decorator Marietta Hines Gomez is famous for the tremendous elegance of her nearly monochromatic rooms, often in multiple shades of off-white.

You can wrap yourself in a favorite color by painting the walls and ceiling and adding a rug, furniture, pillows, drapes, and accessories in many shades of that same color. Avoid extreme color contrasts—it is a harmonious, "wrapped" look that you are after. The subtle variations in tone and textures will keep monotony at bay.

"Black is for contemporary rooms."

Touches of black are wonderful for pulling disparate elements together, no matter what the style of the room. Bind a sisal rug in a country room with black canvas edging. A black lampshade, a grouping of elegant black Oriental vases, a single ebony-stained table, and a pair of black wrought-iron candlesticks are like punctuation points in a room. They have less to do with period and more to do with room continuity.

I covered the seat of an antique settee with black vinyl as an unexpected twist in a traditional room, but for daring use of black Donna Karan pushes the envelope. "Painting our entire apartment black was a dramatic thing to do," she admits. "We got the idea when we saw a play with an all-black stage set. The blackness canceled out the architecture, making the actors and the props stand out. We wanted that same effect at home."

Oreo Colors
Bill Blass on the two-color scheme, in this case, rich chocolate and white. Elegant. Calming. Easy to emulate.

Mucho Macho Color

Gerald Schmorn, housewares designer for Christian Lacroix, had a craving for a violet couch in his study. To tame and defeminize it, he painted the walls chocolate brown and laid on the leopard.

The White Idea

This collection of blanc de chine nineteenth-century Chinese pottery and antique creamware is dramatically set against a contrasting white. Nothing is more elegant than white on white.

Color It

• Color is portable. Put a vase of lilies on a table and in a flash you've injected a shot of yellow into a room's palette without any commitment. Recognizing that color is mobile and temporary gives you great freedom. And it's mistake proof. If you don't like the way a color looks, just pick it up and move it.

• Use color as an accessory to match your moods. A wooden screen painted shocking pink set against a white wall makes the pink as much as an accessory as the screen.

• Surfaces are manipulated by color—and vice versa. The texture and shape of those surfaces greatly influences how the eye perceives color. The same blue, for instance, will look one way on a smooth wall and another on a stucco wall—and different yet again on a silk pillow and a cotton one.

Color Partners

Green In nature, green goes with everything, and its multiple shades give it a complex personality. Juxtaposed with red, green is elegant, strong, visually soothing, and not just for Christmas. Tinted with gray, green is restful and soft. Blue with green echoes the most basic color combination—blue sky and green grass.

Yellow Bright yellow can be warmed with oranges and earth tones such as caramel and brown, or toned down with violet. Yellow with red says Provence.

Red When treated as a neutral, red is warm and comforting. Orangey-red is a spicy blend that hints of the exotic. Blue brings out the mysterious, dreamy side of red.

Blue Pale blues amplify a sense of space, are soothing, and together with white create a fresh, breezy look that is pretty in any room. Deeper blues become jewellike when complemented with reds or greens.

Cool Black

Donna Karan calls her black bedroom "calm, comfortable, and sexy. The cashmere makes you want to lay down all over everything and the black is ultimately calming."

Neon Rocks

A collection of antique Vaseline glass looks modern beaming against a mahogany chest.

TEXTURE AND PATTERN

Stained Panes

This twist on stained glass uses a brightly colored plastic plaid shade.

A room should feel as good as it looks. Texture energizes a room and softens the often hard lines of modern life. Just as a painter manipulates the size of a brush stroke, its thickness, and the direction of the paint to create texture, so can we use fabric, objects, and wall treatments to generate a rich juxtaposition of textures in a room.

You might not realize that texture and pattern are related, but pattern gives a grain even to a smooth surface mimicking roughness and nap. Pattern in area rugs, plates, vases, paintings, decorative boxes, wallpaper, drapery, slip-covers, and pillows gives richness and intensity to a room. Textures like chenille, velvet, corduroys, bamboo, sisal, and sea-grass come with "built-in" pattern. Use these textures to contrast with the cool sleekness of wood, glass, leather, or stone.

Stone, wood, and grasses bring us back to the earth. Mix them in their natural form with the traditional textures of carpets and upholstered furniture. Add a fountain in a bedroom, a flat of grass inside the fireplace during nonwinter months, a bed of stone in a corner, bowls of potpourri or lemons in every room.

Texture Meets Pattern
Maxine de la Falaise puts together an old Chinese hamper, gilded flea-market finds, a carved wooden lion, stone, and glossy red paint.

Mix and Stir
Designer Maxine de la Falaise's texture recipe: stone floor, gilded wooden chest, glass, and brass.

It Is What It Is

Philippe Model knows what to leave alone and what to embellish. These walls, untouched as he found them, tell plenty of tales. The real beauty of Model's salon walls was in the moldings—so he played them up in blue and violet.

Screening Material

These clay chimes prove that almost anything that can be hung or strung on the vertical can make for original and attractive screening material.

"Richly textured materials, such as Oriental rugs, brocades, damasks, and jacquards, belong in formal rooms."

Formal is a label and labels are restricting. Learn to live without labels and watch what happens. Favorite fabrics can be everywhere you go so you can enjoy them. I've filled my beach house, for example, with a mix of rich fabric pillows. Persian rugs look wonderful layered over sisal or terra-cotta. Velvets and brocades complement rattan furniture. Conversely, cottom ikats on antique mahogany chairs break the formality of a dining-room table.

"Muslin, printed cottons, glazed chintzes, and gingham checks belong in casual rooms."

These fresh-looking fabrics can keep "serious" furniture from looking staid and breathe life into stuffy spaces. Remember—innocence mixed with sophistication is devastating. Bill Blass, for one, uses muslin on museum-quality furniture.

"Sleek surfaces belong in modern rooms."

Smooth works everywhere. Satin, silver, brass, glass, mirror, chrome, Lucite and aluminum, marble, high-gloss floors and furniture, silk, and ceramic—all bring a clean, cool feeling to a room, no matter what its style. Mix modern slick black vinyl and inexpensive fabrics in formal settings.

"Rough surfaces are for rustic country rooms."

Stone, brick, raw wood, terra-cotta, linen, roughly woven fabrics, and natural fiber floor coverings are warm and inviting. They beg to be touched. Warmth is desirable in every room, unless you are going for a "my house is a museum" look.

"Patterns confine and define and are difficult to mix."

Plaids with florals, checks with stripes, small paisleys with ikat prints—mix it up. The only rule left is to try to use colors in the same intensity—and have one or two colors repeat throughout the room. These common colors can weave dozens of prints together. And keep the patterns different sizes—for example, small checks and bigger floral prints or vice versa. In one room I will pick out colors from plaids to use for solid-colored pillows.

"Complex patterns are for large rooms only."

As it turns out, small rooms are perfect for patterns, which give a sense of grandeur and drama to even a tiny space. The luxurious use of pattern goes against the tired advice to go pale and plain to make a room look bigger. Play with scale. To the eye, lavish can mean large.

"In smaller spaces, keep contrasts in texture to a minimum."

This rule is based on the idea that texture equals bulk and bulk takes up space. But texture doesn't have to be bulky. It can be delicate.

"Heavy pieces of furniture should be upholstered with heavy fabrics."

In other words, use velvet, leather, tapestry, and woven wool on couches. This makes as much sense as telling everyone over size 6 to not wear a silk blouse. High contrast is never a mistake.

"Avoid using equal amounts of opposite textures, such as heavy and light, or a room will lack focus."

Out of focus is okay. Something slightly off-kilter or blurred around the edges is always more interesting than everything right on. Odd numbers are somehow always more fun than even ones. Decorating drowns under the weight of too much fussing: It is not a science. Make your own measurements.

Square One
Play with patterns of durable flooring squares. Here, alternating vinyl linoleum and vinyl floral canvas have created a checkerboard.

Syrian Symphony
This bedroom has painted cedar wood walls with original eighteenth-century decorative paintings with Syrian motifs that exude texture and sensuality.

Turn Up the Texture

• Give punch to a boxy room with a richly patterned rug, sofa, or upholstered wall.

• Small accessories like plates, vases, and tabletop sculptures create movable pockets of texture and pattern. Rotate them as the spirit moves. Make your home a living environment that reflects your moods.

• Lacquer and satin finishes give texture to walls with their sheen.

• Opposites attract. They bring out the best in one another. Soft with hard. Shiny with rough. Patterned and plain. A one-note perfume is never as intriguing as a daring blend. So it is with textures and patterns. The more you mix, the more you'll get it right.

• Leave a wall patchy. Let it show you what it's made of. Let plaster be a little crumbly. Coat plain drywall with a coat of drywall compound to make it look like plaster. Grit is good. Mix some sand into your paint and give a new rough edge to a smooth wall.

• Go timeless. A room can look great if you use lots of wood and stone, sliced granite, chunks of quartz, and slabs of marble. Leave wood floors uncovered. Rustic benches, wooden trunks, and farm tables bring an earthiness to a space. So do matchstick blinds, raffia fringe, chunky woven baskets, twine, rope, netting, and old quilts. Use fabrics with dimension created with small mirrors, sequins, or shells. Their appeal is universal and mixes with any style or any period.

Not a Scarf in Sight

One designer threw away the rule book and covered a traditional love seat in a psychedelic Pucci print, not unlike Jackie Onassis, who used Liberty scarves to make throw pillows.

Home Stretch

A couch runs the length of a room filled with a mélange of prints, patterns, colors, and textures.

WA LLS

Whimsical Walls

Almost any idea can be translated with paint.
Parisian artist Pierre Gripperay painted on
"panels," then glued on scallop shells.

Walls really *do* talk—about you. What you do with your walls reveals a lot about the kind of person you are. Are your walls loud or quiet? Playful or serious? Are they cushioned with fabric or coated with copper?

What can you do with a naked wall? It is the largest blank canvas in your home, a personal envelope waiting for your stamp. Today's walls are more versatile than ever before. They are able to open and close, lower and raise up, light up and cool down.

Mirrors Multiplied

Bill Blass loves mirrors and uses them in multiples throughout his home. More is more when it comes to little mirrors of various periods mixed on a wall.

Textural Tapestry

Antique tapestry like this is hard to come by. Duplicate the look by stenciling or hand-painting designs on artist's canvas. Seal and age with tinted glaze.

"Carefully sand and prime walls before painting them."

There is beauty in imperfection. Play up a wall's flaws and blemishes. Exaggerate them. Celebrate, don't conceal, cracks. After stripping wallpaper, think about leaving the wall as is. Leave the traces of past paint jobs or the wallpaper glue. This creates age and character, gives lineage, and hints at past lives. A compulsively prepared wall can end up looking lifeless. If you're painting, try scratching up the dry paint with steel wool or fine sandpaper to add a little world-weariness and turn up the charm.

"Raw plaster or stucco walls are only for country or informal rooms, not traditional ones."

Plaster has coated walls for centuries and it's still a good choice. The appeal of raw plaster and stucco is a strong one. They're warm, mellow materials, and they're loaded with texture for the taking. The earthiness of these materials can bring even the fanciest room down to earth where it belongs.

"Paint finishes are less expensive than wallpaper."

Wallpaper was originally used during the nineteenth century because it was cheaper than paint, and it's still a great buy. In one sweep, it can add pattern, color, and texture to a wall. In addition to paper, you can find reasonably priced luxury fabrics like damask, velvet, or suede on the Internet or at fabric houses that carry seconds. Theatrical supply shops have well-priced burlap, corduroy, linen, and felt.

Wallpaper doesn't have to be wallpaper. Take a page from the celebrated Scottish architect Charles Rennie Mackintosh. He covered his dining-room walls with plain brown paper (the kind you use to wrap packages for shipping). Leave it as is, stencil it, decorate it with painted freehand designs, or dab on silver or gold paint for highlights.

"Wallpapering means covering a wall edge to edge with glued-on paper."

Wallpaper these days no longer means what it used to—rows of video monitors, for instance, are video wallpaper. A wall covering of photographs serves as wallpaper, as do maps . . . or photocopied family photos, botanical prints, large groups of posters, playing cards, postcards, gift wrap, or old menus. These don't even have to be glued—they can be framed and hung or attached and positioned with double-sided tape. The added plus? You don't have to deal with matching seams and patterns.

Coquillage
Gripperay made candle sconces from mussel and scallop shells. To the right, each shell used in the apartment's decoration is identified.

Family Wallpaper
Why stash those family photo albums? Live with the great moments. This is my kitchen wallpaper.

Disappearing Doors

Interior designer Pierre Passebon covers his walls with artwork in identically colored frames. "I hang pictures to make the door disappear when it's closed."

Following page

Excavation

Fashion designer Philippe Model stripped the paper from the walls of his apartment in Paris and loved what he found in one corner. To duplicate it, he methodically rubbed on color, put up paper, then stripped it off leaving shreds and exposed chunks of glue.

Ways with Walls

• Hang reversible curtains on the lower half of walls. Use moiré on one side, for a formal look, and a plaid on the other side for a more casual look. The atmosphere of the room can do a quick change this way by flipping the curtains over— use small hooks or rings to hang the fabric on the wall.

• Paint metal washers from the hardware store in metallic copper and affix them in a geometric pattern to a wall. Or cover walls with sheets of copper.

• Consider a process called *stucco veneziano* which trowels a layer of wax on the wall to give it a luminous quality.

- Apply parchment paper or sheets of Chinese ceremonial paper to walls with wallpaper paste.

- Hang inexpensive cheesecloth or cotton all around a room from rods hung at ceiling level for a sumptuous, soft look.

- Line walls with floor-to-ceiling bookcases. To create the look of recessed cases, continue them around the windows and doors.

- If you live in an architecturally deprived space, purchase personality—wainscoting, cornices, crown moldings.

- Use lengths of grosgrain ribbon, gilt, mahogany framing, or painted molding to finish off walls or to create decorative panels on a plain wall.

- Make thin, inexpensive wallpaper richer by giving it a coat of matte polyurethane varnish or a plain or tinted glaze. This will give your paper an antiqued quality.

- Instant Italian villa. Use stucco, either white or pigmented, with a great Tuscan color like yellow ochre, dusty rose, or peach. Go a step further and stencil with baroque or rococo designs. Or paint on fake columns, cornices, a wispy grapevine, or a collection of marble busts.

- Stick squares of felt, suede, or leather onto a wall with fabric glue. Use a checkerboard design using two or more colors, making sure the squares butt up to each other tightly. To add a more polished look, glue on thin piping or ribbon to conceal the joined edges.

- Buy one or two rolls of expensive wallpaper. Use it to create panels, then border them with gilded molding.

- Add plaster molding detail, readily available on the Internet or by catalogue in shapes as small as two-inch bees and one-inch daisies or as large as one-foot Grecian urns and ornate flowery patterns.

- Concrete-patterned wallpapers give texture to walls without the weight of real concrete.

- Drape yards of gauze or muslin over a mirrored wall. Pull it back here and there with tie-backs to play with space.

Wallpaper Without Wallpaper

Cover walls with . . .

- Plates. New ones, old ones, any you love.

- Ceremonial masks.

- Fans.

- Old metal or wooden tools, numbers, signs, or letters.

- Picture frames left empty.

- Mirror images. Mirror real pottery or ceramic vases by displaying them on mounted shelves or pedestals, then stenciling images of them on the wall behind them.

- Funky finds. If it speaks to you in some way, find a place to hang it.

FLO ORS

Jungle Chic

A bear skin and other animal prints mix well when layered on other patterns in the Zadora family's Fifth Avenue apartment.

As the largest uninterrupted surface in any space, the floor sets the tone of a room.

Warm it up with texture and color. Cool it down with hard surfaces and steely or transparent neutrals. Treat it like a blank foundation on which to showcase your movable parts—the furnishings and accessories that are going to make your tableau. But whatever you do, know that the floor can be manipulated to contrast or complement your design scheme.

Industrial-strength materials being used today such as steel and rubber have a high-tech look that can instantly update an interior. Marvelously sensuous underfoot, leather flooring is the height of luxury. I layer carpets of woven plastic, one over another, mixing patterns and colors. There are more choices than ever. You can even design your own rug on the Web with a few mouse clicks.

Look Down

Borrow an idea from a Parisian artist who has embedded square glass blocks into the ceiling of his atelier, flooding the room with light *(right)*. But a glass surface brings light to both sides, and so the glass ceiling is also a glass floor. The result is a kitchen floor that glows underfoot *(left)*.

"Linoleum and rubber flooring are for high-traffic rooms only."

Linoleum and rubber are big news again. Their terrific variety of colors and their durability make them attractive and practical for any room.

"Coir, rush, jute, sisal, and sea-grass are for casual interiors."

These floor coverings, which are all made from the natural fibers of plants, blend with any period or style. They have an earthy, timeless appeal that gives texture and, sometimes, pattern to a floor. Contrary to rumor, most of them are soft, easy on the feet, and very durable.

"Redecorating means a new floor."

Or revitalize your existing floor. As in all decorating, sometimes what you think you need is already there. Sand down and reseal your wood floor. Stain or dye your carpeting, or cut it into area rugs and have the edges bound. Paint or stencil existing tiles.

"Wood isn't for kitchen floors. Use tile instead."

This rule has led to lots of aching backs. While ceramic tile is beautiful and easy to wash, it's very hard. It doesn't give. This makes it tough on the legs and back when cooking for long periods of time. It is also cold (something to think about if you have young children). Go with the grain. Woods like oak, maple, and birch are durable, hard-wearing, and have enough play in them to make them easy on the body. Treat these woods to an oil finish to make them easier to care for. Or use Pergo, a laminate that looks like the real thing but is virtually indestructible. If you're sold on ceramic tile, use it. Just add a good rug or mat in front of the sink and stove to cushion your feet.

Felt Floor

Squares of felt whipstitched together are soft underfoot and become wall-to-wall carpet.

Stairway to Heaven

The bleached wood floor of this elegant foyer, combined with the rosy surface of the walls, brightens, softens, and creates freshness. Against this pastel backdrop, the lacy banister becomes a life-size piece of filigree jewelry.

Floor Choices

• Concrete floors can be warmed up with paint, polish, or stenciling. They also can be scored with patterns or set in intricate patterns with tiles (or flat-backed clay or beads, or bits of broken tiles or dishes).

• Rug remnants can be finished with piping.

• Turkish and Persian rugs have been prized in the West for centuries, since Marco Polo brought them back with him from his travels. Add a modern twist to these timeless rugs by casually layering them.

• Terra-cotta tile, a favorite flooring in the Mediterranean, Mexico, and India, can be configured in many patterns. Sets of squares, diagonals, or herringbones can be made with square, rectangular, diamond, hexagonal, and octagonal tiles. Once the tiles are set and grouted, they can be left naturally rough, polished, or sealed to resist moisture and stains. For a European look, place hand-painted tiles at intervals to act as accents.

• Ceramic tile is synonymous with Spain. Glazed in bright colors, such as yellow, red, and blue, and polished to a high gloss, they are often arranged in tight, highly decorative patterns.

• Leather is the greatest extravagance possible for flooring. Leather "tiles" are made of steer hide cured with vegetable tanning and dyed. They can be embossed or printed with pattern. The gaps between the tiles are usually filled with Carnuba wax.

• Cork is soft, warm, and available in many colors and grain patterns. It is sold as tiles that are laid over a sheet cork underlay.

• Mosaic tiles can be played with to give a new take on tradition. Bette Midler uses mosaics to "paint" Hawaiian designs and sayings like "Aloha" in her house.

• Glass blocks can be set in concrete to make a honeycomb pattern. Or round, lenslike glass blocks can be set in a polka-dot pattern. Glass is used to open up a space and bring in light from the level below.

• Aluminum, steel, or copper sheets or tiles can be nailed or stuck down over an entire floor or part of a floor. Metal sheeting is available in many patterns and finishes (anodized, satinized, and bright, among others).

• Zinc was commonly used to surface bars in Paris during the nineteenth and early twentieth centuries, and Parisian bars are still often referred to as "zincs." Zinc is a soft metal, which makes it very good for bending and molding to cover wooden stairs making a sleek metal "runner."

• Linoleum today is flexible, easy to cut, and it can be laid out in intricate diagonals, squares, and rectangles, basket-weave designs, tumbling blocks, key squares, and more.

• Rubber is available in many colors and raised patterns such as herringbone, checkerboard, wavy wide, narrow ribs, and studded. It is warm, soft, quiet, and rough.

Tiles on the Rise

A checkerboard painted tile pattern climbs
the stairs by decorating the risers.

LI GHT

Shadow Play
Subtly painted "shadows" stretch across the ceiling and onto the walls, playing with illusion in this Paris bedroom.

The way a room is lit determines how we feel about it and how we see everything in it. Textures, color, accessories, *all* are sculpted by the type of lighting we choose. Lighting highlights and accents. Or, by its absence, it diminishes. Lighting strongly affects the ambience of a space. The brighter a light, the more exposed we feel. The softer it is, the more protected and calm.

To Bette Midler, "Light is everything. Light, light, light . . . gotta have light. . . . I can't stand to live in dark places." Midler is a huge fan of Swedish painter Carl Larsson. "He brought light into Swedish homes plunged into darkness by short days," she says. "His use of light was magical and it inspired me in how I decorated and lit my house."

Mirrors, lamps, sconces, chandeliers, and windows have all become more than just light sources. These light sources have been reinterpreted and revolutionized. Light can be manipulated by mirrors, semi-gloss or gloss paints, even by the color and size of a light bulb. Indeed, with a plug and a light bulb anything can be made into a light source. Or pull the plug once in a while and remember to make use of the brightest light of all—the sun.

Firelight
Mirrored tiles and pieces of gold and silver leaf on Bette Midler's chimney turn a structural feature into a decorative one. Artist Nancy Kintisch designed the fireplace screen and the mosaic hearth. "We had Swedish Mania for a good five years," says Midler. "I have a real weakness for Carl Larsson and this fireplace is based on one of his designs."

Amazing Lace
Sunlight picks out the intricate patterns and beautiful workmanship of an old piece of lace I sandwiched between panes of glass to camouflage the brick building across the way.

Overleaf
Light Flight
Ceiling lights don't have to be centered. They can literally sprout wings and fly across the ceiling.

"Lamps on either side of the couch or bed should match."

If you want a motel-room look, stick to this rule. Otherwise, use lamps that you love, whether they match or not. They don't have to be the same height, same style, or same period, and the shades can be entirely different, too.

"A lamp is a lamp."

A lamp or light source is where you find one. Make a lamp from an alabaster urn, a large conch shell, an earthenware jug, old pillars, vases, a perfume bottle, an old teapot, or a sugar bowl. A large glass funnel turned upside down makes a great hanging fixture. So does the top of a glass cake plate, as Agnes Colmar uses throughout her Paris apartment. I made a sconce from the arms of a statue. Urns of alabaster or any translucent material can be electrified for dramatic uplighting.

"It has to have a plug."

Some of the most beautiful lighting is not controlled by a switch. Discover natural light sources. Mirrors bring light into a room. So do windows, skylights, and glass building blocks. Turn off a lamp and light a candle. Use a cluster of paper lanterns or a pair of antique sconces. Play with light and shadow. Rediscover the purity of sunlight.

"Don't use an overhead light in the bedroom."

Overhead light can be garish, but it depends on the light itself. French designer Gerald Schmorn uses a star-shaped chandelier by Tom Dixon in his bedroom, and has painted shadowy stripes down the walls to play with and manipulate light. Dimmers have also changed the old rules of lighting, allowing overhead lights to emit a controllable glow. Florence Grinda, an executive in Sotheby's Parisian office, uses dimmers on every overhead fixture and table lamp in her house. She says, "I can't stand harsh light. Soft light makes people look beautiful, so that is what I use."

Grow Light
Another sculpture turns over a gilded leaf to become a sconce.

Vines for the Divine
Bette Midler's window was sandblasted with leaves by designer Joe Murphy to mirror the foliage outside.

Light Is Where You Find It

Open your mind to new sources of light and you'll find them where you never thought to look.

• Metallic paints add and reflect light on moldings, banisters, and trim.

• Gilded surfaces bring light into a room—existing light is reflected by frames, statues, and bits of gold costume jewelry used as decorative hardware on furniture.

• A gold colorwash can illuminate a wall. Silver paint or metallic powders ranging from bronze and copper to aluminum, pewter, and burnished iron can also be particularly helpful in a windowless room or hallway.

• Use fabrics woven with gold or silver threads or decorated with tiny mirrors or shiny beads.

• A collection of lusterware china hung on a wall or displayed on a shelf or in a cabinet brings light to a room.

• Translucent light-diffusing screens and doors transmit light through a space.

Beam Me Up

• Use pink bulbs or a pink shade in the bedroom or dining room. Pink flatters the complexion and gives a rosy glow to the room. And remember: Two 40-watt bulbs provide kinder light than one super-wattage one. French antiques dealer Nathalie Bellanger paraphrases Marlene Dietrich's famous saying, "You can be the most beautiful woman but nobody will know it if you are not correctly lit."

• To simulate sunlight, try a mix of incandescent, halogen, and fluorescent bulbs.

• Install a skylight or glass blocks into the ceiling or walls.

• A halogen torchère gives pure, sunlike light that's not too yellow or too cold.

• Remove the handle from an inexpensive Oriental parasol, turn it upside down and mount it over a nondescript ceiling fixture to give it exotic style and soften the light with the lacquered paper. This looks great in a hallway or foyer.

• Place multiple lanterns in a small space for dramatic lighting.

• Use a large fixture in a small space to add drama.

Tree of Light
In the apartment of Nathalie Bellanger, a sculpture branches out into a new role. Christmas tree lights can illuminate anything to form a sculpture.

Lean on Me
Mirrors don't have to be mounted on the wall. For a more casual look, lean mirrors and artwork against walls; this also keeps them portable.

Light Times Light

Multiply light. The same fixture, repeated over and over, makes a mobile of light.

Made in the Shade

Canvas screens adjusted to the light are ever-changing mobiles. Overhead screens like these are used in conservatories to adjust the amount of light the plants get.

Mirrors

Mirrors attract light like a magnet. They play with it, bounce it around, and make it dance. One source of light becomes two, becomes three, and on and on.

To explore the effects of mirrors:

• Create a mosaic of tiny mirrored tiles on a chimney wall.

• Think big. Lean an oversize mirror against the wall in the living room or dining room. Or create a wall of mirrors by leaning mirrors of approximately the same size against a wall.

• Mirror the insides and top of a window frame or the step risers on a staircase.

• A large mirror on a wall opposite a window will reflect the outdoors, bringing it inside.

• Convex mirrors create points of light within a room.

• Location, location, location. Before hanging a mirror, study what it will reflect. A mirror panel in a fireplace creates light in a black hole. Choose a spot that will highlight a great view—a painting or a chandelier.

• A mirrored wall should be used the same way a nonmirrored wall is. Hang paintings, a collage of photographs, drawings, clocks, empty frames, and other mirrors over it.

• Place one mirror parallel to another to give an *Alice in Wonderland* effect.

Find the Window
Designer Maxine de la Falaise created a puzzle of light in Sarah St. George's house in France. It is hard to tell where the windows and doors are because mirrors were used to manipulate the space.

Bubbles of Mirror
Winding along a dark staircase, convex mirrors add dimension and light.

Overleaf
Light My Fire
"In Paris apartments there are many fireplaces. Some work. Some don't," observes designer Gerald Schmorn. "Is there anything worse than that black hole you see when a fireplace isn't working? I took apart a Venetian mirror and had it mounted on a wooden frame made to fit my fireplace. It reflects light this way and the hole disappears. Even a simple mirror leaned inside of the fireplace would work."

FUR NITU RE

On Fire
Josie Natori gives fiery passion to a tufted
antique chair and suggests a new definition
to the traditional flame stitch.

Traditional furniture can be anything but. Upholster a precious museum-quality antique in plain four-dollar-a-yard muslin, calico, or a Navajo blanket. Or use dress fabrics like silks, organza, or cashmere to dress up a couch. Paper a chest of drawers with sheet music or old love letters. Appliqué flames on a traditional sofa, as Josie Natori does in her Paris apartment.

The way we use furniture has evolved in much the same way that our use of rooms has. Flexibility and practicality are our prime concern now, and looking pretty is not enough. Furniture has to feel as good as it looks and it should be multifunctional. A headboard should slide open for storage. Tables and chairs should roll to where they are required.

The dining room set is dead. So are the bedroom and living-room sets. They're out of touch with the availability of great eclectic designs. Mix. Opt for the unconventional. Pick and choose individual pieces that appeal to you. This personalizes space and makes your home different from anyone else's.

Bale Out

Fashion designer Cynthia Rowley says she has a Green Acres sort of relationship with her husband. "You know, darling I love you but give me Park Avenue. He's very outdoorsy and I'm a city-holic," she says. To bring a touch of country into their very cosmopolitan living room Rowley a friend to make an ottoman out of a bale of hay.

Think Mink

A Lucite stool cloaked in mink rosettes by designers Heather Hoyt and Alison Diamond. It is the juxtaposition of low- and highbrow that makes this work.

Preceding pages
Unification Theory

Different chairs are unified with whimsical hand-painted designs based on a nature theme.

Rules to break

"Think in sets."

Safety in pairs is boring. Aim for asymmetry. End tables *don't* have to match. Use an oval table on one side and a square one on the other. Or don't use tables at all. And you don't have to face sofas and love seats in sets. Go with a love seat and two chairs or a chaise longue. Or use four or five very cushy, comfortable armchairs arranged in a circle.

"Upholster within the character of the furniture."

Be contrary. The contrast of fancy and plain makes the form and beauty of antique furniture come alive! Think of using gingham and muslin, blue denim, white canvas, simple calico, even a cut-up woolen blanket or old linen tablecloths on antique furniture. Gerald Schmorn, a designer for Christian Lacroix housewares, used a colorful Pucci print on his couch.

"Chairs and couches form seating areas."

It doesn't have to have legs to sit on it! Consider big plump pillows, ottomans, and old blanket chests. Covered Zenlike flat cushions are creeping into the most formal settings. Donna Karan loves sitting on the floor. "It's an Asian sort of thing," she says. "It's very grounding and casual and I find that when we entertain, people love sitting on the floor—it makes them feel very at home. In my home, everyone plops down first on my silk beanbags."

"Dining room chairs should match."

"A flock of one kind of chair" is something to be avoided, says interior designer Richard Keith Langham. "When you mix chairs, you can either keep to a similar silhouette, or totally mix them up any way you want to." Surround the kitchen or dining-room table with mismatched chairs dressed up with interesting braid, cord, or fringe hot-glued along the seat bottoms. Old banker's chairs painted glossy black look sensational. Or use dining chairs on one side of the table and a bench, love seat, or easy chairs on the other side. Or use the same chairs in different woods or with differently upholstered seat cushions.

"Woods should match."

Mixing woods and finishes creates style and interest. Don't feel locked into one type of wood. Look in your backyard and see the different types of trees living side by side—oak, pine, beech, maple. They don't clash with one another and neither will your furniture. Mix in some glass, whitewashed, lacquered, and painted pieces as well.

"Every living room needs a coffee table."

Not long ago there was no such thing as a coffee table. If you don't want one, don't have one. Use two small square tables side by side instead. Top an ottoman with a tray for holding drinks. Use a stack of art books as a table. An old window, a wrought iron garden table, an ornately carved Indian bed, or a piece of an iron gate can be fitted with legs and topped with glass to make a coffee table.

Out of the Rec Room
The lowly beanbag reinterpreted in raw silk. Informal doesn't have to mean inelegant.

Second Life
My mother loved this nineteenth-century American bellows so much we still use it as a coffee table.

Furniture has to feel as good as it looks and it should be multifunctional.

Take a Towel
An exquisite antique secretary desk plays against type and holds towels.

Fearless Furniture

• Top a sawhorse with a slab of glass or marble to make a dining or sofa table. Or use an old wooden door.

• Replace usual cotton canvas seats and backs of director's chairs with a great heavy upholstery fabric or tapestry. Then edge with braid or glass beaded fringe.

• Use fabulous fakes with pedigreed pieces. Lucite furniture doesn't apologize for being man-made. It is what it is— practical, modern, clean, infinitely useful, and easy on the eyes. Designers Heather Hoyt and Alison Diamond topped a Lucite stool with mink rosettes for a French Designer's Showhouse held in New York.

• Old metal office furniture fits in anywhere, anytime, and instantly updates interiors. Or use modern updates, as fashion designer Cynthia Rowley did. "I bought my dining-room table from an industrial catalog that had everything from furniture to forklifts in it," she says. "I spotted this great cafeteria table that had stools attached to it. It had such a cool look, I knew I had to have it." There's a lesson there—search out unusual sources for furniture and accessories. Showcased in a residential interior, commercial furnishings can look fabulous.

• If you want a coffee table, look for one with built-in shelves to stash books, newspapers, and magazines.

• Call them ottomans, hassocks, whatever . . . they're everywhere. Like all good things that go out of style for a while, they've come back with a vengeance. Slipcover one with a few yards of fake fur or remnants of velvet. Leather Moroccan ottomans are usually sold folded flat—ready to stuff with old clothes or newspapers to make them grow fat and sturdy.

• As libraries go digital, traditional wooden card catalogue cabinets are being tossed. Catch one and use it to store CDs or tapes.

• Use deep, glass-fronted china cabinets or secretary desks to hold books, towels, wine bottles, stacked quilts, bolts of fabric, or a TV set. In the kitchen they can hold table linens, even canned goods.

• Old painted furniture with chipped and peeling paint has great charm—but give it a coat of amber shellac to seal it.

• Instead of upholstery sample books, look for vintage fabrics in antiques stores, yard sales, on travels, or in your attic. Exchange off-the-rack for one-of-a-kind.

Living on the Edge
Once a table for an antique basin, this Oriental artifact is now a narrow wall shelf.

Cover Me
Break with tradition and upholster antique furniture in an unexpected fabric. This chair is covered with pieces cut from a Navajo blanket.

ACCE SSO RIES

Dip in the Sea

Large shells can be used as fruit bowls or serving bowls—they make the ultimate one-of-a-kind accessory.

A house isn't a home until it's filled with your favorite things. An old crock here. A teapot there. Your mom's Vaseline glass. Magnifying glasses picked up from your travels. Textile print blocks. A fistful of shells. Anything and everything that you enjoy looking at.

Artists surround themselves with objects that inspire and feed their creative side, and so should you. You probably have a collection already without realizing it. Walk around your house and find one. Gather all your vases. The plates that are too good to eat off. Those beautifully colorful foreign banknotes that you will never spend. Things made from the same material, or of the same shape, color, subject, or texture. Stuck away in a drawer, it's just clutter—displayed, it's a collection.

A collection can be made of anything that holds special meaning for you, whether priceless Fabergé eggs or pebbles gathered on a walk along the beach. Some of the most striking accessories come directly from nature—driftwood, a shell, a bird's nest. Architect Len Morgan says, "I'm not judgmental about where something came from. If it looks good and means something to me, I use it. I have a sand collection. I gather sand from places I've been to like Thailand, Monte Carlo, the Bahamas, San Francisco, and put it in handblown glass jars. Then I label the jars to remind me of where it came from and of the good time I had in that place."

High Hats
These one-of-a-kind hats designed by Bes Ben in the 1940s are now collector's items that look great displayed on a wall like works of art.

Crystallize This
Contrast the sleek and refined with rough surfaced minerals, creating a yin and yang for the ages.

"Collections should be valuable."

Put presence over provenance. "If both the expensive and the inexpensive are, in their ways, first class, they can be perfectly harmonious," declared interior designer Billy Baldwin.

Jackie Onassis made table displays of Greek worry beads, a dried mushroom on a branch, an Egyptian cat cast in bronze, and a piece of black twig coral together. A *Vogue* fashion editor I know arranges all her ivory brooches on her living-room end table. Jackson Pollock and his wife, Lee Krasner, mixed arrangements of shells and driftwood. My friend, Katel Le Bourhis, the creative director of Louis Vuitton Moët Hennessy, pins her collection of family military medals to her lampshades. Bette Midler turned her collection of vintage Hawaiian fabrics into pillows.

"Less is more."

Only if you like a spare look. Some people love lots of things around them. The same object repeated again and again makes a strong statement. It could be marble or cast plaster busts, silver fruit, little tin cups . . . anything. There really *is* strength in numbers.

"More is more."

Not if you *don't* like lots of things around you. There is great power in the number one—as in one great thing prominently displayed. It could be a giant urn or mirror, an exceptionally large piece of furniture, anything that commands undivided attention.

Shore Thing
Barnacles as a flower vase. This would be a terrific toothbrush holder, too.

Glass Forest
Ambassador to Norway Robin Duke mixes glass balls with pinecones for year-round display.

Things made from the same material, or of the same shape, color, subject, or texture,create a story.

Fan Dance
Fans can float across walls, mix colors and textures, overlap them, and rotate them in different directions.

Lovable Stuff

• Plants, flowers, fruits and vegetables, a goldfish, or a bird are living accessories. They breathe life into the most stagnant space. And they're movable. For less upkeep, use glass flowers, porcelain, silver or beaded fruits, and animal figurines. For real punch, mix the real with the fake.

• Sometimes it's the shape of the object that counts. In wood, marble, porcelain, or glass, obelisks make an impressive tabletop display. Globes, alabaster orbs, marbles, a collection of old baseballs, or perfectly round oranges are worthy accessories. Round is comforting.

• Touchable things are inviting. A craggy rock, a rough piece of driftwood, the sleekest glass paperweight, a smooth marble egg, furry toss pillows, chunks of crystal, fossils—these are objects we naturally want to handle.

• A footed bowl is an indispensable accessory. Fill it with colored marbles, coral, beach glass, jeweled fruit, Christmas tree ornaments—it raises anything you put in it to dramatic heights.

• Move accessories frequently to different locations within a room or from room to room. An object in a new spot becomes new again.

• A vase is where you find it. Flowers look marvelous in a beautiful old can, a cocktail tumbler, a trophy, a shell. Some things to collect now: old hotel silver, aluminum bar and kitchenware, anything of Vaseline or mercury glass, coffee pots, Buddha heads, fifties or sixties glass accessories, old olive oil jars, foreign packaging, junkyard finds, silk-screen blocks, small vintage pocketbooks, antique intaglios, pastry molds, travel mementos. The search is endless.

• Think plastic. New colors and techniques have made it new again. Plastic is best when it's not trying to be something else like wood or marble. Pick plastic that's proud of being man-made.

Quirky Is Good
The real with the fake can be a visual joke. Why should my glorious Judith Leiber eggplant purse stay in my closet? I perched it on top of a bowl of green apples.

Surprise
A mercury glass ball nests on a couch.

DISPLAY

Get It?
The way you display objects can tell a story . . . or a joke. Photographer Ivan Terestchenko does both by putting a crown on this statue of Lenin.

Stuff—we all have it. We can group it or pare it down. Highlight it. Create themes. Link colors and shapes. Mix the functional with the ultra luxurious.

Live with your favorite things where you can see them every day. Arrange them until you find a configuration that speaks to you. You'll know it when it happens.

Friends
The simple necessities of country life celebrated by Bill Blass.

Butterflies Are Free
As an alternative to the traditional mounted butterfly box, jewelry designer Andreas Zadora displays them in flight between two sheets of Plexiglas.

Basic Black

Instead of mixing colors, a collection of black biscuitware makes a powerful statement.

Hang It Up

Philippe Model has transformed his country French chairs into wall art and, at the same time, solved his storage problem while creating a great look.

"Objects of value create the most impressive display."

Not true. Even the most mundane objects can be elevated to importance, whether isolated against a great white surface or grouped in multiples. Good things are worth repeating, even dried weeds in simple ceramic flasks.

Build a great wall of china with mismatched tag sale plates, tureen or sugar bowl covers, or ironstone platters. Or isolate one of something you like in a corner or in a fireplace. Stones, shells, driftwood . . . everything and anything you like.

"Art should be showcased on a plain unpatterned wall."

Layering patterns gives a room depth. If in doubt, extra-wide mats surrounding a picture supply a little breathing space between the pattern on the wall and the subject matter of the art. White plates or collectibles pop against a wallpapered wall. Pictures or paintings displayed on bookcases add perspective to a room.

"Match the size of the artwork to the size of the wall. In other words, small wall equals small art, large wall equals large art."

Bananas . . . don't be afraid to aim for the unexpected. An outsize framed vintage poster filling up a sliver of a wall becomes important "wallpaper," as does an entire wall covered top to bottom with framed mirrors or black-and-white photos. Or go the opposite way. Try leaving a large wall clean and uncluttered to exaggerate its size. Or hang one small mirror smack in the center of it to act as a pinpoint of light.

"Group objects according to style, or period, or media."

This is credo if you're a museum curator. Or if you are very specific in what you collect. If you are a theme collector, throw this rule out. Flowers, animals, landscapes, or portraits done in various media are an exciting way to display a favorite subject. For example, if you're a cat lover and want to display an eighteenth-century Staffordshire cat figurine, a modern framed black-and-white postcard of a cat, the clay cat you made in camp as a child, a Steuben glass cat, a reproduction ancient Egyptian cat figure you bought at a museum, and a flea-market wicker cat basket together.

"Functional isn't pretty. Hide from view the things that make a household run."

Form and function often are a beautiful team. Glassware, plates, wooden chopping bowls, olive oil bottles, tea tins, and boxed foods can look wonderful. Treat a chair as sculpture and hang it on the wall. Place costume jewelry in a pattern on a side table or line up an infantry of boots in an entrance. Umbrellas and canes stacked in a tall cylindrical *anything* look sophisticated.

Don't be afraid to look "lived in." I never felt welcome in the home where my friends' mother vacuumed as soon as we walked on her carpet.

Play Dress Up
Belgian designer Kathleen Missoter displays a dress on the wall as a spontaneous artwork.

Blue by the Dozen
Group by shape and color and stagger the heights. My collection of blue vases varies in age, value, and country of origin.

Don't be afraid to look "lived in." I never felt welcome in the home where my friends' mother vacuumed as soon as we walked on her carpet.

Hands Up

I thought my collection of these gloves, which belonged to the Duchess of Windsor, were special enough to form their own sculptural grouping with a little help from hand mannequins.

Good Bones

This table in Cynthia Rowley's home offers a fascinating inspiration for one's own furniture—to dangle beads or balls or glass prisms or anything.

Shhh

White plates are used to quiet this dining-room wallpaper.

The Art of Showing Off

• Contrast color, texture, or size when displaying objects. Learn from nature. Things in the natural world never match. Some things tower over others. Colors don't follow rules about where they should or shouldn't go. Rough lies down next to smooth, shiny and dull live side by side.

• Relax when arranging objects on a tabletop. The more precisely placed things are, the more untouchable they look. Collections should be shared. Guests will feel intimidated by a perfectly arranged display. See the beauty in unusual juxtapositions. Try for a sense of luxe minus fuss.

• Be playful, not predictable. Try something quirky. A porcelain or silverplated piece of fruit mixed in with the real thing, a priceless Fabergé egg in a real bird's nest, old perfume bottle tops in a fine silver bowl, glass balls lining the perimeter of the room.

• Go casual . . . lean artwork against walls and stack books on tables and chairs, or even on the floor.

• Use maps, line drawings, and black-and-white prints to give a sense of calm. Manipulate overscale lithographs, posters, and oil paintings in vibrant colors to create a focal point.

• Put anything silver on top of a mirrored surface.

• Hang one of anything beautiful or interesting inside an empty, ornate picture frame or a bunch of them over a window or door.

• Place leaves, foreign bills, antique playing cards, or photos under glass on a chest of drawers, vanity, or coffee table. Tuck photos or postcards into the frames of mirrors. Special photographs should be a part of life, not tucked away in a photo album that's hardly ever opened.

• Flaunt it on fabric. Photocopy a favorite artwork and transfer it to pillow tops or curtains using heat transfer paper sold in craft and better copy stores.

• Even a bare, interestingly shaped branch in a jar looks noble when downlighted with a simple fixture placed above it. The less-is-more look embraces simplicity.

• There's magic in mixing periods, styles, shapes, and sizes. Vary the heights to create a staggered effect. Stacked books make an instant pedestal for a small object.

• Don't dot. Resist trying to accent with small accessories. Gathered on a shelf, mantel, tabletop, or windowsill, they will gain strength in numbers.

• Don't fall into the "tulip trap." Did you ever see tulips pop up one at a time precisely a foot apart in someone's garden? They've been planted that way. Experienced gardeners always plant in clusters of three or five or more for a natural look. Follow that method when displaying objects. Try to avoid placing accessories on shelves or tables like soldiers lined up for battle.

Multiplication
Bill Blass's white cameos, butterflies, and flowers show the power of multiples.

Virtue in the Vignette
I created a wall treatment with hats and heads as the theme.

Architectural Finds

Until this century, deeply carved architectural trims—ranging from columns and capitals to banisters, crowns, corbels, mantels, arches, and crowns—were mostly the property of the rich and royal. They were associated with huge manor houses or châteaus. Now, these elements can be found in junkyards, flea markets, and salvage yards. If not there, there are reproductions. Brass grilles from the thirties and forties or iron fences make great headboards. Lightweight plaster casts can be painted or antiqued to look as if they are hundreds of years old. Look for discarded gingerbread trim like old wooden corbels from demolished homes, hotels, or restaurants. They make great shelf supports. Or treat them as sculpture by placing them on a modern oblong or square column. Architectural elements give a sense of history to new rooms.

Open Jewel Box
Candace Chabannes takes her bracelet collection out of the
jewelry box and onto the coffee table.

Reality Play
Marcia Riklis plays with perspective by layering a painting over
her bookcase and by mixing the real with the faux.

ECLECTICISM

Smile While You Soak

Maxine de la Falaise put a painting surrounded by a collection of tiles by this bathtub. So much personality, it makes you smile.

Forget what you've been told about what goes with what, sticking to one period, one decorating style, or one color thread. It is all boring. Karl Lagerfeld once told me that great style, whether it be about clothes or homes, cannot be all salt or all sugar . . . mixing both is what satiates the style taste buds.

Real chic comes from mixing it all up, expensive with bargains, antiques with new. The Moroccan vase you get as a wedding gift can look great with all your American department store furniture. Old French faience can fit comfortably next to flea-market glasses. Loosen up and let your intuition take over. If you don't like the way something looks, you can always change it.

PLAY. Put a funky lamp on a pedigreed table. Modern, colorful pillows on a Victorian velvet settee. Or cover a beanbag chair in richly colored Thai silk in a room of more formal wooden furniture. Alter the spirit of a room with a surprise, a jolt.

What do you do if you want to use your grandparents' old breakfront, you're deeply attached to an old spindle chair that got you through school, you've bought a lot of upholstered pieces during one uncontrollable spending spree online . . . and your living room's ended up looking a little grannyesque? Modernize it with a glass coffee table and some sleek wrought-iron accessories and lamps.

On the other hand, maybe you've out-sleeked yourself with too many minimal parsons tables, leather chairs, and slick surfaces? Try messing things up a little. Add heat and punch with pillows in warm colors, throws, a pair of ornate lamp fixtures, or a console in gilt woodwork.

Filling up your living space is like painting on a blank canvas or assembling an outfit. You are building a look—your look. The advantage of being eclectic is that it gives you the broadest of palettes, one that allows you to dabble in cultures, styles, and periods.

One of my mentors, Bernadine Morris, former fashion editor of *The New York Times*, told me the key to style is never looking like you spent hours putting yourself together. The same goes for decorating a space. It shouldn't look too matched, too decorated, too precise. Fashion designer Cynthia Rowley agrees. "The worst thing is to have everything perfectly appointed," she says. And Calvin Klein equates modernity with relaxation: "The role of modern design is to make living in a complex world—where even time has become a luxury—easier, more relaxed; it goes beyond trends. Mix casual with formal and work with modern textures and different weights and forms."

A great room is the sum of its parts. Look at your possessions with a fresh eye and see the possibilities in what you have. Isolate objects against a blank wall to really look at them. Group them in a new way. Mix media—glass with books, wood with metal. Dare to dare. Real luxury is living with what you love, not with the best money can buy.

Still unsure of just how eclectic you can be? Let a legendary arbiter of style guide you. Madame de Pompadour searched the ruins of ancient Rome and returned to Paris with cartloads of architectural artifacts to mix with her Louis XV furniture. Follow her lead. Get out there and hit the local junkyards and flea markets for great stuff to blend in with what you already have.

Eclectic Girl

The daughter of jewelry designer Andreas Zadora lives surrounded by all her favorite things. An antique settee and formal fireplace get friendly with contemporary frog furniture.

Mix It Up

In my entry foyer, a nineteenth-century chandelier from a hunting lodge, a 1940s settee, and a contemporary artwork featuring a giant birthday cake live happily together.

The Eclectic Spirit

Fashion designer Cynthia Rowley offsets the classic beauty of wood panels and a carved marble fireplace with modern sculptures and furniture. Even a pair of drums is at home in this room.

"Decoration means coordination."

Resist the off-the-rack look. A modern sculpture on an antique dresser plays with new and old. Whether it is a stone fresco hung above a primitive Chinese wooden side table or a rugged log cabin centered on a crystal chandelier, unexpected juxtaposition makes you see things in a whole different way. French antiques dealer Nathalie Bellanger says: "Mixing makes a room that's like a mind, filled with many memories."

If you faithfully follow one style, how can you possibly get it wrong? Well, you could end up with a room that looks like it came from a hotel chain. Different styles should play off one another. An eclectic home is a personal timeline, an autobiography. Use objects bought on travels, inherited pieces, and gifts you've been given to tell the story of who you are.

"To be eclectic means anything goes."

There is a definite line between eclecticism and chaos. A room can take on an eclectic look by using subtle contrasts as well as bold ones. A contemporary home filled with classics or an historical one filled with contemporary ones automatically has an eclectic spirit. But it's certainly possible to create an incoherent space by jettisoning all organizing principles.

Start small—with galvanized metal chairs pulled up to a rustic country dining table or a sleek halogen lamp on a Chippendale desk. Mix shiny with rough, urban with earthy, provincial with palatial, old with new, the found object with the treasure. That's what eclecticism is all about. But there is safety in some uniformity. Keep one color of wood in a room of different period furniture. Use neutral walls to showcase varied forms of art.

Time Warp
Parisian interior designer Pierre Passebon uses antique furniture and textiles with contemporary art to highlight the beauty of handmade objects throughout the centuries.

Eclectic Calm
A rich mix of elements doesn't have to be busy—it can be quiet and calm.

Fusion
Slick contemporary surfaces contrast with rough ancient sculptures, shells, and fossils.

Cyntillating
Old finishes and new ones, modern and antique, in Cynthia Rowley's house. Similar colors unite the different periods and shapes.

Real luxury is living with what you love, not with the best money can buy.

Bettina Patina
In Bettina Gabetti's bedroom, an unusual antique wooden table from Hong Kong, treasured for its patina, bridges the centuries next to a contemporary bed and an Andy Warhol.

The Eyes Have It

Laurence Baumer uses color to pull together an eclectic mix of colors, periods, styles, patterns, and textures.

Crystal in the Rough

Contrast can be stunning. Against the backdrop of the rustic log cabin, the sleek crystal chandelier pops out like a pearl in an oyster shell.

Break the Mold

• In the dining room, mix antique chairs with a contemporary table. Or vice versa.

• Use a glass-topped modern metal table in front of an antique sofa. A simple modern piece juxtaposed with an ornate old piece brings out the beauty of two eras.

• Hang a work of abstract art in a traditional room.

• Let line, color, and shape unify objects. Centuries come together when emphasis is placed on similarities rather than differences.

• While you might want to mix with abandon, certain periods and styles do marry particularly well. Good blends include Victorian, art nouveau, and eighteenth-century French pieces; Scandinavian modern, Shaker, and Japanese; English Regency and Chinese; contemporary and Japanese or Chinese, seventeenth-century Italian and art deco. But don't hesitate to make other combinations. A bit of deco with Shaker. Or Scandinavian modern with Chinese. In moderation almost anything can be decorative punctuation.

• Midcentury modern, the furniture and accessories from roughly the 1940s through the 1950s, is highly collectible now. Its finishes are light, its lines are simple and clean, and practicality is its premier concern. Think Heywood-Wakefield, Russell Wright, Knoll, Charles and Ray Eames, and Eero Saarinen. Much of their work is being reissued today if you can't afford the originals. Even one piece of midcentury modern will give a newness to a traditional room.

GLO BAL STY LE

Tourist Attraction
Venetian masks, a Chinese lacquer piece, and an American Steinway piano chair spice up a guest bedroom in my Sagaponack potato barn.

Who needs a passport when you can design a carpet from Nepal over the Internet, order Chinese wedding chests from a catalog, and find imported Indian textiles or Indonesian teak in mass-market stores? It's never been easier to mix in ethnic touches or experiment with a look you've never tried before. Today the world is our market. In addition to buying on the Web, I never go anywhere without an empty duffel bag to fill with irresistible items I might find at a local flea market or in a remote village.

Integrating global finds is like living with a three-dimensional travelogue: instead of just socking away mementos in photo albums that I look at once a year, I'm living with my treasures. Ethnic and global artifacts help us to get away from the cookie-cutter. An African mask placed on a sleek glass-and-steel modern table adds new perspective, as does a leather Moroccan saddlebag as an ottoman with a modern sofa. These elements close the gap between cultures and between centuries. Look at the lines of your furniture. They are probably simple, clean, and uncluttered. Play with them by using imported pieces carved with elaborate twists and turns, intricately embroidered textiles, vivid colors, and lush textures.

The Ming Thing
Fashion designer Josie Natori uses Oriental porcelain as a centerpiece on her dining-room table and parades figures in front of an ornate gilded mirror on her mantel.

Transglobal Guest Room
French sheets, Indian blankets, Peruvian dolls, and a French lamp in my country guest room.

"Ethnic or global pieces should be showcased as a collection and treated as artifacts."

Whether a room is traditional or modern, the recipe for an engaging space is to mix cultures as functionally as possible. Take that piece of great Thai silk or African woven raffia and make it into a pillow to spice up a traditional couch. Mix in pieces of bamboo with modern or traditional furniture. Chinese furniture, no matter how ornate, goes with any other style. Don't be afraid to integrate the most rustic of travel mementos. Display Indonesian textile blocks on a fine piece of English furniture.

"Keep to one style or period when using ethnic pieces."

The fun is in the mixing. Everything and anything goes. But be selective in your choices. The idea isn't to make your home look like a Moroccan souk or Indian bazaar. Subtlety works. Use imports to spice up, not overpower a room. A group of Chinese figures can share the same mantelpiece as two French period vases. Or use the drama of one exceptional piece as a focal point—an African fertility figure, a large Oriental vase filled with bamboo stalks, a pair of antique Indian candlesticks, or a pair of Chinese black lacquered chairs. Mix new and vintage, reproduction and ancient artifacts. What matters is the shape, line, color, and character of the object.

I Only Have Eyes for You
French jewelry designer Laurence Baumer hung a greatly magnified photograph of an insect over a tribal mask he thinks it resembles. Ancient ceremonial figures stand guard.

Syrian Symphony
French interior designer Pierre Passebon's bedroom has an eighteenth-century *à la polonaise* bed with the original fabric. The eighteenth-century chair is covered with the original toile de Jouy.

Satays of Style
Indonesian wall hangings transformed into towel racks bring
the exotic into the bathroom.

Watch Over Me
An Indonesian serpent is mounted to make a headboard in
journalist Suzanne McDonough's bedroom.

Everywhere Meets West

The Orient is a constant influence on today's interiors. We respond to its sense of calm in our stressful world.

A room infused with the quiet order of the East is luxurious, detailed, beautiful, and never busy, understated elegance

at its most tranquil.

The current interest in all things Asian is reminiscent of the rage for Oriental design during the eighteenth cen-

tury. Then, furniture, walls, accessories, and textiles were decorated with Chinese-inspired motifs called chinoiserie.

The style was popular in the American Colonies, especially in wallpaper designs and painted murals. The French mixed

chinoiserie with their own rococo Louis XV style. In England, the influence of China was seen in the furnishings made

by Chippendale.

Form and Function Need No Passport

• Chinese wooden chests, lacquer boxes, and carved wooden bowls bring warmth to a room.

• Large clay pots, rice baskets, and wooden trunks make great end tables or nightstands.

• Orchids, bonsai, jade plants, and gnarled willow branches ooze charm.

• Oriental rugs work well with any style of furnishings and add color, pattern, and a splash of cultural diversity underfoot. They look great overlapping one another underneath English Regency to postmodern pieces.

• Hang a kimono as wall art or use Indian saris as curtains, table coverings, or bedspreads.

• An East Indian hand-carved standing screen or an old carved Mexican door can be placed behind a couch to replace hung artwork on the wall. Wood carvings, ceramic works, masks, metalwork, and handmade crafts can all be isolated as works of art that humanize modern interiors in particular. What may look like street bric-a-brac while you are in foreign lands really can become sculpture the minute it is placed on Lucite blocks.

• Hand-embroidered tapestries create texture and give depth to a room. Drape them over the arm or back of a sofa, hang them over a mantel or balustrade, or use one as an area rug.

• Pieces of mahogany or teak furniture with iron hardware, inlaid with beads, mirrors, or jewels, are a great accent.

• Consider animal hides to cover an ottoman coffee table. Use decorative tile to cover a side table. Use handcrafted metal or raffia curtain tie-backs. Or bamboo stalks as curtain rods.

• Many cultures have small shrines for prayer and spiritual reflection. It is very personal and interesting to create your own spiritual corner with religious artifacts, candles, small sculptures, even beautifully shaped stones and bits of driftwood. You really can make a special place of quiet within the busiest household.

Grass Roots

Stark and minimal showcases global. An ebony Balinese wedding couple flank my ivory-colored fireplace, which I accented with a flat of grass.

Roll Call

Chinese figures stand at attention under a contemporary painting in Bettina Gabetti's apartment.

SPACE

In Praise of Space
Oversize windows, simple furnishings, and a totally
unadorned fireplace create a celebration of space.

"Space has to become your own personal artistic experience." So says fashion designer Donna Karan. To most of us, lots of space is the ultimate luxury. Grand space is liberating. It makes us feel limitless. But to many of us, a small, cozy room is complete comfort. If your rooms are physically just the right size for you, you're very lucky.

Here are some ways to stretch or shrink space to make it more compatible with your physical and psychological needs.

Fabricate
Make a room within a room. Create private niches with drapes.

Cornered
An oversize globe and mirror make a small corner big.

"Keep furniture small in a small room."

Filling a small room with small furniture emphasizes the small size of the room. Think big. Play with space and visually expand it. Use oversize furniture. Big couches. Hefty tables and sculptures. Large paintings and lamps.

In the diminutive bedroom jewelry designer Andreas Zadora created for his daughter, an oversize doll house fills the center of the room, giving the illusion of a much bigger space.

"Keep accessories small in a small space."

One great piece is always better than a lot of mediocre ones. Don't think of this as a poverty of riches but as the luxury of less. Calvin Klein says, "Paring down is actually more difficult than adding embellishment—embellishment can hide flaws. With fewer elements, what's not essential is immediately discernible and interrupts the rhythm and mood of the environment." In fashion, doing less exposes and emphasizes the bare essentials—from the seams to the zippers. In home design, editing puts the focus on details such as the way the piping on a chair is finished or the way objects are placed.

"Paint a small room white to make it look bigger."

If you regard smallness as a problem that has to be fixed, this is a valid rule. But smallness can be cozy. Many of us feel more relaxed in a small room because we feel more sheltered, more protected. Play up a small room by going in the opposite direction. Exaggerate the smallness. Paint the walls a *dark* color, like chocolate brown, deep burgundy, forest green, or rich blue. These colors advance rather than recede. They push outward and wrap themselves around you.

Breathing Space

An architectural frieze is framed by bare space so as not to distract from its beauty.

Clutter Free

Bill Blass uses oversize accessories and furniture to make a big statement in a small room, in pale tones accentuated with black. The large mahogany column is floating architecture used to divide the space. "I hate the word cozy," he says. "Anything that is cooling and evokes serenity appeals to me."

"Very large rooms are cold. Use furniture, pattern, and accessories to warm them up."

To many, lots of space is the ultimate luxury. Flaunt it. Revel in the openness by keeping it clean and uncluttered. Resist the compulsion to fill up a large space. Fashion designer Bill Blass uses supersize mirrors, furniture, and accessories to emphasize the large proportions of his rooms.

"A too-tall ceiling should be visually lowered by painting it a dark color."

To many people, there's no such thing as a too-tall ceiling. They see lofty ceilings as pure drama and glamour. But if you feel overwhelmed or somehow dwarfed by the height, bring the ceiling into scale with the rest of the room by using tall furniture or indoor trees. Hang art slightly above eye level, paint ceiling beams decoratively, or use wainscoting to pull the ceiling down.

I consciously crafted a place near the top of my double-height ceiling to position a sculpture, purposely emphasizing the height as a design element.

Royalty
A castle big enough for a queen grows out of the floor of a tiny bedroom. The canopy pulls the eye up and makes a miniature turret for a little girl.

"I Am Not Small!"
I like to use big, bold accessories even in my smallest room.

Overleaf
Lower the Beam
Painting the wooden beams visually lowers the ceiling and cozies up this bedroom by Maxine de la Falaise.

Making Rooms Look Bigger

If you don't want to go with the flow, there are ways to stretch space visually. Sleights of color, texture, pattern, and accessories can do it.

• Use open "leggy" furniture to keep space open and airy.

• Shadows chop up space. Coax as much natural light into a room as possible.

• Pull furniture toward the center of the room, away from the walls, to create an intimate conversation area. In the bedroom, float the bed in the center of the room.

• Uplights, torchères, and wall sconces illuminate the ceiling and reflect light back into a smallish room to make it look bigger.

• Hang pictures of landscapes or detailed abstracts that pull the eye into the distance—a great trick for giving a room more depth.

• Stick with smooth surfaces such as tile and glass, which reflect light.

• A lot of pattern pulls a room in. Little or no pattern does the opposite—it opens up space. And if you cover everything in the same pattern, it will seem to disappear.

• Keep window treatments simple. A simple shade, shutters, or a swagged sheer is enough. If you use drapes, hang them high, right up to the ceiling and down to the floor, the way Calvin Klein has done in his New York City apartment.

• A pale color repeated room to room creates a seamless flow in a small home. It pulls the eye through hallways, around corners, and past architectural shortcomings.

• Periodically weed out the contents of rooms. Be ruthless. If you don't love it, move it out. Len Morgan says, "Don't show all your booty. Put some things in the closet for a while." Calvin Klein shares this view. "Good design involves an editing process incorporating purity of form, quality of elements, scale, and proportion that is well-considered."

• To "raise the roof" use low furniture and built-in platforms. Or paint a design or apply a broad wallpaper border along the baseboard—the expanse of wall above the border creates an illusion of height.

• Curvilinear shapes such as circles, cones, and spheres give movement and openness to a small, tight space. A round glass coffee table, a collection of globes, even a fabric pattern featuring circles or dots, will bring roundness into a shoe-box-size space.

• If possible, remove the interior doors between rooms to keep a flow going. Or replace wooden doors with glass or translucent doors.

• Use a semi-gloss or high-gloss finish on walls rather than a matte one. This will reflect light and give the illusion of a grander space. Ditto for ceilings and floors.

Set Afloat
Floating the bed in the middle of the room creates the illusion of limitless space.

Making Rooms Look Smaller

Sometimes a large room appears cold and unfriendly and needs to be warmed up.

• Len Morgan advises, "Create several different smaller areas within a large room." To make private spaces in a big room, use drapes. Hang them from the ceiling and pull to the side with tie-backs. Or tent an entry room and hang a chandelier. This creates a warm, intimate space that draws guests inside.

• Use plenty of pattern. Oriental rugs, patterned wallpaper and French country printed cottons make a room shrink visually.

• Heavy soft textures add warmth to a space. Use faux fur, chenille throws, woolen rugs, velvet pillows, tapestries hanging on the walls, lush draperies.

• Rather than scattering little tables, small chairs, or stools around the room, use big pieces of furniture in dark woods like mahogany or lacquered chinoiserie pieces.

• Strong colors on the walls and the floor will wrap you up in warmth.

• Highlight the perimeters of the room with a wallpaper or painted border trim.

• Draw attention to beams, structural columns and other architectural elements.

• Place books or baskets underneath tables. This will fill in bare spots and make use of space that is usually wasted.

Raise the Roof
Drapery pulls the eye up and gives extra height to this small entryway by designer Jennifer Ellenberg.

Cocoon
An ambassador's house in the south of France breaks up a large bedroom by closing in sleeping nooks just as Thomas Jefferson did at Monticello.

MULTI FUNCT IONAL SPACE

Relaxing Read
A bathroom/library. Good lighting makes it easy to soak in the tub with a good book.

Space is precious. Don't let a room's name tell you what to use it for. Forget the name. Use rooms for the way you really live. Let a living room become a media room. A closet or hallway change into a kitchen. According to fashion designer Donna Karan, "I dine, do yoga, watch TV, and entertain everywhere. There are no more rules. People live a luxuriously casual life now." In the East, every room except the kitchen and the bathroom, are considered living rooms, dining rooms, and bedrooms. Screens are used to alter space.

Work and Play
In my dining room, a sliding glass door opens to accommodate large parties. When not used for dining, the second room is my husband's home office *(left)*.

Overleaf
Three in One
A kitchen in Paris cooks, serves, and cleans clothes all at the same time. Artist Benoit Tschieret says, "This building dates to the 1930s and was built as subsidized housing, which purposely combined the bath with the kitchen. I decided not to change it to keep the spirit of the original building. And, it's actually very nice to be able to socialize when I'm taking a bath."

"Bedrooms are for retiring."

A bedroom is much more than just a place to sleep. Many people like to eat, read, watch TV, exercise, and work in the bedroom. A chaise and a good reading lamp along with a generous table/desk can transform a bedroom into a work space as needed. Buy a headboard that slides open to reveal bookshelves. Put a desk in the armoire. Add a small refrigerator for late-night snacks or a glass of orange juice first thing in the morning. Use back-to-back dressers or bookshelves to create a private space for exercising.

The ultimate dual-function bedroom is one created by fashion designer Peter Nygård on his own island, Nygård Cay, in the Bahamas. Attached to a cable above the ocean, "By the push of a button, it will lower itself down to the water so you can take a swim with the dolphins," Nygård explains. "Push the button and go up and have breakfast!"

"Living rooms are for entertaining. Make it the most formal room in the house. Put the TV somewhere else."

Living rooms are no longer museums. The on-your-best-behavior living room that was off-limits to anyone but guests is gone. Fashion designer Cynthia Rowley remembers, "My mom always said she hated a living room that looked as if it should have velvet ropes around it. I grew up in a house where nothing was off-limits and I use that same philosophy now with my own family and friends."

Living rooms should be for living. Find furniture that gives you storage for books, games, toys, and media equipment. Look for ottomans that open. Tables with removable tray tops for eating, or breakfronts with pull-out shelves for desk work. Living rooms can be used for a variety of functions, with changes in lighting, flooring, furnishings, and even color denoting changes in function. Screens are terrific for creating a smaller area within a larger space and their portability makes them perfect for temporary changes. I keep a television in an antique armoire that enables me to conceal it when I use the living room for entertaining.

"Dining rooms are for dining."

When no one is eating, a dining room can look like a furniture showroom. Push the table against the wall to use as a desk and turn your dining room into a home office. Stash paperwork and stationery in a chest of drawers and keep the computer in a breakfront or armoire, or on a rolling table that can be placed behind a screen when necessary. Put up bookshelves and make the dining room into a library. Attach a triangular piece of wood in a corner and pull up a chair for an instant desk. Add upholstered seating and a TV that can be camouflaged behind a screen so that you can sometimes use this room as a sitting room.

Towel Tuck
A sliver of space neatly stows away rolled towels.

Before and After
Chanel's marketing director, Marie Louise de Clermont, has a large beautiful bathroom overlooking the Palais Royal in Paris. When a dinner party is being planned, voilà! A cushioned board is placed over the tub to serve as a banquette, a table and chairs are moved in, and it's a dining room that seats twelve!

Book Mobile

Bookcases in this antiques store have been transformed into sliding doors. The shell-back chairs are nineteenth-century Italian.

Hidden Storage

Calvin Klein's headboard slides open to reveal extra shelf space for reading and writing materials.

Two for One

- Making space multitask.
- Use tracks along which you can glide screens, paintings, or flat-screen TVs to camouflage or manipulate room function according to need.
- Room dividers can be created using large paintings, opaque glass, bookcases on casters, or even Venetian blinds hung from the ceiling.
- Use "softscaping" to create rooms or to separate space less permanently. Hang sheer curtains or lightweight mosquito netting from tension rods to make a graceful, temporary divider. A sheet of plastic or fabric or muslin printed with oversize photographic patterns can achieve the same effect.
- Convert a large closet into a home office, using a built-in shelf or a small desk. Hang additional shelves to hold storage boxes and files. Put casters on baskets to make portable files.
- Transform a foyer into a library by lining the walls floor-to-ceiling with bookshelves.
- Use area rugs or a change of lighting to signal a change in function within a single room.

Cramped Quarters

In this small apartment a closet has been transformed into a kitchen and part of the bedroom walls into a pantry.

Please Come In

One apartment dweller wanted a country house mudroom in her New York City residence. The solution from designer Peter Marino: Make over the elevator vestibule into a cosy cubby. Bottled water, scarves, gloves, tissue, and Chapstick are handy as family members come and go.

Screen It

Screens are miracle workers. They mold, shape, and privatize space. A fundamental element of the Eastern interior, screens bridge spaces or separate them.

In addition:

• Screens add pattern and texture to a room.

• Opaque screens called *shoji* divide space without cutting off light. So do screens made from beveled glass or old windows or doors with glass panes hinged together. Small, private spaces are created with the use of screens in Japanese homes. Places to meditate, have tea, and display art can be easily kept apart from the rest of the room with a screen.

• Bamboo blinds mounted on the ceiling can be raised or lowered to open or close off a space.

• Rolling screens, similar to the ones used in hospital rooms, are now available for home use and give you the freedom to reshape your space in any way at any time.

• Architectural elements such as old shutters, columns, and porch posts can be used as screens.

Bogus Books
Computer equipment is tucked into a wall and a TV is hidden behind a screen that looks like a bookcase.

Room with a View
A tabletop screen made of beveled glass divides space without blocking the light.

NEGLE CTED SPACE

Not Your Mother's Closet

Bring cloak closets out of the closet by honoring them with decor befitting a living room, from chandelier to fleur-de-lis–stamped walls.

154

Any room in which you spend time deserves to be beautiful. Too many of us have boring bathrooms. Horrendous hallways. Dull landings and laundry rooms. We figure they don't matter because for the most part they're not seen by guests. Stop treating yourself as a second-class citizen. Every part of your home should please you. Corners. Ceilings. The space under the stairway. Windowsills. Balconies. These are notoriously neglected by most people.

It only takes a little thought to accent the ignored spaces in your house by accessorizing them with clever visual surprises . . . the painting hung over the doorway to stretch the eye and the room upward . . . a statue teetering on the top of a tall piece of furniture . . . maps, fishing rods, and pottery decorating the ceiling.

You can use every sliver of space in your home. I'll show you how.

Now Showing
A flat-screen television hangs from a ceiling track.

His and Hers TVs
What better way to be noninvasive with technical things than to sink them into the wall? In a neglected space over the doorways of this library, two people can watch different programs with individual audio headphones.

"Decorate bathrooms practically with fixtures and furnishings customized for bathrooms and use nonbreakable accessories only."

Nonbreakable can be confined to the shower. The rest of the bathroom doesn't have to be devoid of interest. Silver, porcelain, crystal, or wood objects look great in the bath.

"Don't waste time or money decorating a laundry room. Nobody sees it."

Flash! Any room where you spend time should be visually pleasing. Even the lowly laundry room can pamper you by looking good and reflecting your personal style.

"Corners and ceilings should be left bare so that they don't detract from the rest of the room."

Why can't they *add* to the room? Corners are pockets of space that can be put to use as work or display areas, while a ceiling's decoration can be the topping on a beautifully decorated room.

"Landings and hallways need, for safety's sake, to be left clear."

While these spaces should be easy to navigate, they can be decorated so that the "journey" is as exciting as the destination.

Figure This
Georgette Mosbacher positions figurines as visual surprises above a door and lets them teeter on the tip of a tall piece of furniture.

Out of the Cupboard
And onto the ceiling. Florence Grinda hangs plates and illuminated glass grapes on her kitchen ceiling.

Bathrooms

Bathrooms have long been oases of privacy. These days, that fact is celebrated and exploited in dozens of ways. Add a padded garden bench, chair, chaise longue or even a small sofa. This gives a place to sit—for getting dressed, giving haircuts, or polishing nails. That it's a bathroom doesn't mean it can't have a wonderful little table for holding makeup, toiletries, and so forth, or a bookshelf, magazine rack, display cabinet, or curio cabinet for stacking reading material, a pad, pen, and family pictures.

Bathroom decoration does not need to be different from the rest of the house. Try anything that you'd use in any other room as long as it can't be damaged by humidity. Soft lamplight rather than prepackaged overheads can look great. Add a flea-market chandelier or candelabra. Hand-carved wooden bowls can hold soap, shells, or potpourri. I keep a silver bread basket filled with antique perfume stoppers from the Paris flea markets next to my bathroom sink. Fashion designer Cynthia Rowley puts her towels on an elegant marble pedestal. French designer Agnes Colmer turned a silver ashtray into a soap dish.

You don't have to buy bathroom sets that include matching toothbrush holders, soap dishes, and tumblers in nonbreakable materials to be practical. Use odd saucers, trays, cups, pitchers, drinking glasses, or an old ice bucket to hold soaps, toothbrushes, and combs. Use a covered soup tureen for jewelry or cosmetics. Baskets can store toilet paper or cotton balls.

Silent Butler
Stately accessories like this pedestal bring a sense of grandeur to a bathroom.

Shower Power
Bette Midler decorated the interior shower wall with a beautiful tile mosaic even though it is not a public space.

Laundry Rooms

Since this is your private space, take risks with color and accessories. Assemble a collection of vintage deter-gent boxes or tins on a shelf mounted over the washing machine. Tuck everything into baskets large and small for easy storage. Cover the room with a soft throw rug. Sneak in a little TV or portable CD player.

My laundry room is filled with objects from my travels—straw hats, pottery, copper pitchers. I painted the walls a rich red and stenciled them. I keep my mops in a big old milk can. I used Velcro to attach an inexpensive polyester gold organza skirt to the wash basin.

Landings and Hallways

Nooks under stairs and stairwells can be a functional space for a small desk, a reading chair, a phone. Or, instead of using stairs as a means to an end, make them a destination by treating them like sculpture. Highlight the banisters with ornamentation. Cover the step risers with mosaic tile or paint them with a fun pattern. Staircase landings are natural display cases. I have used them to showcase art, straw masks from New Guinea, Moroccan vases, sculptures, and large mirrors.

Hallways can act as art galleries or functional space, depending on the width. They are great for revolving displays of your children's artwork. Play up the long and narrow shape of a hallway by repeating the light fixture or painting linear patterns. Use this sliver of space to play with mirrors and sconces.

If you have a wide hallway, give it some work to do. Wall-hugging demilune tables with pairs of lamps create a spot to place mail or keys. Or put up a chair rail along the center of the wall wide enough to create an architectural ele-ment on which to lean family photos. Put a pretty carpet runner on the floor or checkerboard tiles laid on the diagonal.

Passageway to Practicality
Hallways are taken seriously in this château outside Paris with shelving, important furniture, and chan-deliers.

Communication Center
A giant blackboard in Cynthia Rowley's hallway is used for spontaneous artwork or family messages.

Hallways can act as art galleries or functional space, depending on the width.

Henna a Hallway

Halls can be daring. Here, the henna patterns Indian women draw on their hands have been used to add texture and interest to a simple passageway.

Corners and Above the Door

Make corners and other obscure spots work for you. Fill them with indoor trees, corner cupboards and benches, a grouping of bamboo stalks, or a screen. Fill a corner with objects relating to a favorite hobby or sport—maybe tennis, golf, or horseback riding. This could be the ideal place to show off those trophies, award plaques, or prize ribbons.

The area of wall space right over a door can be a valuable asset to a room when it's decorated. This is where French decorator Pierre Passebon often groups collections of plates. Sybille Denfert-Rochereau has paintings edged in

gilt and framed with molding mounted above the sitting-room doors of her château in the south of France. Bill Blass uses this area for narrow architectural drawings.

Georgette Mosbacher mounted "his and hers" TVs over the two doors in her dining room. "The wall above the doors was hollow and could easily accommodate the sets and their control boxes. It allows two people to be together and watch what they want to watch."

Made to Scale
Bill Blass raises the eye above a narrow doorway with an extralong framed architectural drawing.

Hot Seat
This Parisian banquette has been created to camouflage a radiator.

Ceilings

The ceiling is the fifth wall of a room, so don't overlook it. Ceilings used to be elaborately decorated, ornamented with moldings, often highlighted with contrasting paint colors, or painted with pictorial panels of landscapes, mythological figures, or cloud-filled skies.

Author Georgette Mosbacher draws attention to her library ceiling with an antique map copied onto canvas and affixed to the ceiling. She says, "My ceilings are high and decorating them is a very good way to pull the eye up and keep the ceiling in scale to the rest of the room." Jack Hemingway kept his father, Ernest's, fishing poles on the ceiling of his Idaho home, while Sotheby's executive Florence Grinda displays an extensive pottery collection on hers. A flat screen TV can be easily hung from a ceiling. If it's put on a track it can be moved to accommodate viewing from different parts of the room.

See the Ceiling
Georgette Mosbacher had an old map photocopied on canvas and decoupaged to the tall ceiling in her library.

Jump out of the Box
A small, boxy room draped and turned into a tent, by designer Odile de Schietere, carves a cocoon by tenting a room and lowering the ceiling.

IN DOORS OUT DOORS

Patio Pottery
Large ceramic chinoiserie pieces are sturdy enough for outdoor use.

TOWELS

Break the boundaries. Bring the outdoors in and take the indoors out. Architectural gems like porch posts, fences, corbels, gates, and bits of Victorian gingerbread become sculpture in the context of an enclosed space. Birdbaths, fountains, metal window casings, and wrought-iron benches give weight to interior landscapes. Likewise flats of grass, bowls of live moss, sundials, and garden statuary breathe fresh air into indoor rooms.

Turn the inside out by using patios, porches, decks, and gardens as outdoor rooms. Experiment with pillows, throw rugs, pottery, and candlesticks. Make the ground your floor and the sky your ceiling. Build walls with trellises and hedges. Accessorize with urns and statues, pottery and gazing balls. Hang a mirror in your garden. A famous horticulturist put one at the end of his bamboo walkway to make it look as if it went on forever.

Camp Out
Sleeping porches were once a common fixture. Here, ivy covers the walls and the "ceiling," making an outdoor room perfect for catnapping.

Treehouse
Real tree trunks replace more traditional supports in this house and tie it to the surrounding landscape.

Preceding pages
Timber!
The outdoors comes inside in a big way. A real tree trunk surrounded by a fitted bench creates a great place to sit and pull off boots in a mudroom.

Accessorize indoors with antique awnings, terra-cotta urns, pottery, and gazing balls.

Patisserie Past

Furniture designer Maxine de la Falaise uses an awning that once hung over a French bakery's door to bring a bit of Provence to this kitchen.

"Garden furniture is for the garden."

Adirondack chairs, sandstone benches, chaise longues, and weathered teak or wrought-iron chairs can easily be softened and refined for the indoors with overstuffed cushions and velvety throws. Old, weathered pieces with peeling paint bring beautiful patina and texture to a room.

"Garden style is for casual rooms."

Bringing the outdoors in doesn't mean transforming your home into a greenhouse. Small "green" touches relax traditional, formal, and even the sleekest modern rooms. Put an old tool set on the small side table or a bowl of pebbles on the mantel. Use a vintage urn as a planter. Old stone columns can come inside to define an interior entrance.

"Fountains belong in the garden or on the patio."

The sight and sound of falling water is so soothing it should be part of your everyday life. Buy a small indoor fountain or make one by placing a pump in a favorite bowl or vase. Add water, a few plants, and plug in whenever and wherever you want, perhaps centered on an entry table or a side buffet. Or go for a more formal look by setting a fountain in a wall niche.

"Cushions, fine wood furniture, and porcelain pieces are strictly for the inside."

Flea-market furniture and attic finds are easily adapted to outdoor use, because if they fade, rust, or peel a little, it's no big deal. As for the cushions, keep a big basket handy to bring them indoors overnight or if it rains.

Wet Spell
A marbled niche with a sculpted indoor fountain and bowl in this provincial château blurs the boundary between indoors and out.

Swinging
Bring outdoor movement inside year round with porch swings, gliders, and hammocks.

Elsie's Idea

Gerald Schmorn was inspired by legendary decorator Elsie de Wolfe when he put up this trelliswork on his walls. "She did it way back in the 1920s. I updated her idea by using white against red, which gives a very modern, graphic look."

A Leg Up

Old apple-picking ladders bring an open-air feeling to a traditional room. To give a "view" of the outdoors, hang a large-paned window papered with botanical prints where a real window might go.

Garden Plans

Inside

- Collect and display old garden tools and seed packets.

- Flank a fireplace with old porch columns and a window with outdoor shutters.

- Hang an outdoor trellis on the wall or use one as a headboard.

- Use branches as curtain rods and look for root or tree trunk furniture.

- Use window boxes inside. Set on the sill and fill with miniature boxwood or dwarf evergreens.

- Electrify outdoor lanterns, sconces, and old glass oil lamps.

- Consider old store signs and outdoor fixtures such as lampposts and fence finials.

Outside

- Make garden music with wind chimes.

- Create a garden sculpture gallery with stone, terra-cotta, metal, wood, slate, or marble sculptures.

- Use mirrors in the garden, positioned so they reflect flower beds, an expansive view, or a piece of art. Or use mirrored gazing balls set on pedestals or just placed casually on a garden wall or step.

- Use the exterior walls of your house or a fence to display plaques, plates, masks, or sundials.

- Experiment with scale by using one large statue, sphere, or obelisk in a small garden.

- Have fun. Place visual surprises around the garden—a big stone urn on its side, a sculpted hand holding birdseed, oversize stone fruit scattered under a tree, a glass bird in a cage or birdbath.

- Hang a crystal chandelier from a pergola or porch ceiling, or a lantern from a tree.

Hot House
A conservatory is treated here as a living room, with artwork hung on the glass walls, chandeliers suspended from the ceiling, rugs laid, and comfortable furniture used as it would be in any other room.

Gate Mates
Wrought-iron gates at the entrance of this dining room give it a garden-party feel.

Resource List

Accessories

Dishes Direct
www.dishesdirect.com

Gumps
www.gumps.com

Lillian Vernon
www.lillianvernon.com

Pier 1 Imports
www.pier1.com

Red Envelope
www.redenvelope.com

Target
www.target.com

Antiques

Antiquarius Antique Centre
131–141 Kings Road
London, SW3 4PW
011-44-207-376-8781

Ball and Ball
463 West Lincoln Highway
Exton, PA 19341
(610) 363-7330
www.ballandball-us.com

The Brass Knob Architectural Antiques
2311 18th Street NW
Washington, DC 20009
(202) 332-3370

Cobweb
(Moroccan antiques)
116 West Houston Street
New York, NY 10012
(212) 505-1558

Crown City Hardware
1047 North Allen Avenue
Pasadena, CA 91104
www.crowncityhardware.com

Ed Donaldson Hardware Restorations
1488 York Road
Carlisle, PA 17013
www.eddonaldson.com

Historical Materialism
125 Crosby Street
New York, NY 10012
(212) 431-3424

Malmaison
253 East 74th Street
New York, NY 10021
(212) 228-7569

Phyllis Kennedy Hardware, Inc.
10655 Andrade Drive
Zionsville, IN 46077
(317) 873-1316
www.kennedyhardware.com

Salvage One
1524 South Sangamon Street
Chicago, IL 60608
(312) 733-0098
www.salvageone.com

Architectural Remnants

United House Wrecking Company
535 Hope Street
Stamford, CT 06906
(203) 348-5371

Urban Archeology
143 Franklin Street
New York, NY 10013
(212) 343-0800

Yesterday's Treasures
1547 County Road 39
(Route 27)
Southampton, NY 11968
(631) 283-5591

Bathroom Fixtures

Manhattan Castles
(antique bathtubs)
76 East Houston Street
New York, NY 10012
(212) 505-8699

Stone Forest
(hand-carved granite sinks)
P.O. Box 2840
Sante Fe, NM 87504
(505) 986-8883
www.stoneforest.com

Waterworks
(sinks and fixtures)
(800) 899-6757
www.waterworks.com

Closet Supplies

Pearlgreen Corporation
606 West 131st Street
New York, NY 10027
(212) 283-0505

Decorative Finishes and Painting

Natasha Bergreen and Liza Spierenburg
35 East 20th Street
New York, NY 10003
(212) 979-6243

Thomas Eberharter
37 West 32d Street
New York, NY 10001
(212) 239-7413

James Omara
Amagansett, NY 11930
(631) 267-8038

Warnock Studios
3245 Nebraska Avenue
Washington, DC 20016
(202) 537-0134

Photo Opportunity

A close-up of the late Duchess of Windsor's shoe closet has been superimposed on a piece of muslin and used as a room divider in my Sagaponack house. This screen can be rolled up and moved to another location at a moment's notice.

Decorative Trim

Fabric Mill
168C Glen Cove Road
Carle Place, NY 11514
(516) 248-8799

M & J Décor
983 Third Avenue
New York, NY 10022
(212) 704-8000

Fabrics

Decorative Vinyl and Fabrics
4527 Glenwood Road
Brooklyn, NY 11203
(718) 941-3326

Cora Ginsburg
(18th-century silks)
(212) 774-1352

Pierre Frey, Inc.
979 Third Avenue, Suite 613
New York, NY 10022
(212) 935-3713

Robert Allen Group
55 Cabot Boulevard
Mansfield, MA 02048
(800) 333-3776
(508) 339-9151

Rose Brand Theatrical Supply
517 West 35th Street
New York, NY 10001
(800) 223-1624

Flea Markets

New York City
Sixth Avenue and 26th Street
Saturdays and Sundays

West Palm Beach, FL
The Fairgrounds
Southern Boulevard
First weekend of the month

Lake Worth High School
(under I-95 Bridge)
Saturdays and Sundays

Paris
Marché Biron
85 Rue des Rosiers
Marché Paul Bert
104 Rue des Rosiers

Marché Serpette
100 Rue des Rosiers

Marché L'Usine
(architectural elements)
18 Rue des Bons Enfants

Floors—Finished Concrete

Buddy Rhides Studio
2130 Oakdale Avenue
San Francisco, CA 94124
(877) 706-5303

Furniture

B&B International Gallery
(ethnic furniture)
601 West 26th Street, 14th floor
New York, NY 10001
(212) 243-0840

Carpe Diem
(lighting and midcentury furniture)
187 Avenue of the Americas
New York, NY 10013
(212) 337-0018

Colin Moore Studio
(metal furniture)
(617) 361-5313

David Rago Modern Auctions
333 North Main Street
Lambertville, NJ 08530
(609) 397-9374

Deco Deluxe
993 Lexington Avenue
New York, NY 10021
(212) 472-7222

Depression Modern
150 Sullivan Street
New York, NY 10012
(212) 982-5699

Ethnic Design
53 NE 40th Street
Miami, FL 33137
(305) 573-8118

Karl Kemp & Associates, Ltd.
(French deco)
36 East 10th Street
New York, NY 10013
(212) 254-1877
www.karlkemp.com

Lin-Weinberg Gallery
(20th-century design)
84 Wooster Street
New York, NY 10012
(212) 219-3022

Alan Moss
(20th-century design)
436 Lafayette Street
New York, NY 10003
(212) 473-1310

Pastense
(1954 revisited)
915 Cole Street, #150
San Francisco, CA 94117
(800) 556-2608
www.pastense.com

Sedia
(20th-century classics)
63 Wareham Street
Boston, MA 02118
(617) 451-2474
www.800bauhaus.com

David T. Smith
3600 Shawhan Road
Morrow, OH 45152
(888) 353-9387
www.davidtsmith.com

Sotheby's
1334 York Avenue
New York, NY 10021
(212) 606-7000
www.sothebys.com

Art on Wheels

Ambassador Robin Duke, who has entertained heads of state for decades, transforms her formal dining space into a room to watch movies. A painting slides back to reveal a TV.

Tucker Robbins
(African furniture)
366 West 15th Street
New York, NY 10011
(212) 366-4427
www.tuckerrobbins.com

William Doyle Galleries
175 East 87th Street
New York, NY 10128
(212) 427-2730

Zanazan
1863 Ridge Road
Champlain, NY 12919
(518) 298-2639
www.zanazan.com

Garden Ornament
Aardvark Antiques
(401) 849-7233

Treillage
418 East 75th Street
New York, NY 10021
(212) 535-2288

Treillage at Gump's
135 Post Street
San Francisco, CA 94108
(415) 984-9276

The Urban Gardener
1006 West Armitage Ave.
Chicago, IL 60614
(773) 477-2070
www.urbangardener.net

Glass
Flickinger Glassworks
(specialty glassworks)
204–207 Van Dyke Street, Pier 41
Brooklyn, NY 11231
(718) 875-1531
www.flickingerglassworks.com

Joel Berman Glass Studio Ltd.
(glass stairs and walls)
(888) 505-4527

Ultra Glass
(tempered glass designs, textures,
and finishes)
9186 Independence Avenue

Chatsworth, CA 91311
(800) 777-2332
www.ultraglass.com

Hardware and Plumbing Supplies
Ace Hardware
www.acehardware.com

Kolson Hardware
653 Middle Neck Road
Great Neck, NY 11023
(516) 487-1224
www.kolson.com

Restoration Hardware
www.restorationhardware.com

Junkyard
Jeski's Market
790 Flanders Road
Riverhead, NY 11901
(631) 727-8877

Leather
Leather Impact
256 West 38th Street
New York, NY 10018
(212) 382-2788
Fax (212) 730-2486
www.leatherimpact.com

Libra Leather
259 West 30th Street
New York, NY 10001
(212) 695-3114
Fax (212) 629-5346
www.libraleather.com

Superior Leather
133 Lexington Avenue
New York, NY 10016
(212) 889-7211
Fax (212) 689-4028
www.repairleather.com

Lighting
Aamsco
(authentic French art deco
and other fine luminaries)
P.O. Box 15119
Jersey City, NJ 07305
(800) 221-9092

Become Illuminated
(888) 605-6243

Carpe Diem
(lighting and midcentury furniture)
187 Avenue of the Americas
New York, NY 10013
(212) 337-0018

Chameleon Antique Lighting
231 Lafayette Street
New York, NY 10012
(212) 343-9197
www.chameleonsoho.com

Chista
537 Greenwich Street
New York, NY 10013
(212) 924-0394

Crate & Barrel
(800) 967-6696
www.crateandbarrel.com

Fabulux, Inc.
(lighting and fixture design)
(718) 625-7661

George N. Antiques
(antique chandeliers)
67 East 11th Street
New York, NY 10003
(212) 505-5599

Grand Brass
221 Grand Street
New York, NY 10001
(212) 226-2567
www.grandbrass.com

Ingo Maurer Making Light
89 Grand Street
New York, NY 10013
(212) 965-8817
www.ingo-maurer.com

Monorail Lighting by Gregory
(sleek, hand-bendable lighting)
158 Bowery
New York, NY 10012
(800) 796-1963

Orleans
68 West Merrick Road
Freeport, NY 11940
(516) 623-8600

Remains
(antique lighting)
19 West 24th Street
New York, NY 10010
(212) 675-8051
www.remains.com

Linen
Domestications
www.domestications.com

Trouville Française
(212) 737-6015

Marble
Wholesale Marble and Granite
150 East 58th Street
New York, NY 10155
(212) 223-4068

Photo Transfer
Showbranphoto
(212) 768-3336
www.showbran.com

Pillows
Françoise Nunnalle
(212) 246-4281
By appointment

Rugs
*Home Decorators
Showcase Catalog*
(800) 240-6047
www.homedecorators.com

Red Thread Trading Company
1905 33d Avenue South
Seattle, WA 98144
(206) 324-9400
www.redthread.com

Screens
British Khaki
62 Greene Street
New York, NY 10012
(212) 343-2299

David Howell and Co.
405 Adams Street
Bedford Hills, NY 10507
(914) 666-4080

M6 & Company
(leather screens)
(901) 452-1810

Muralite
2303 Wycliff Street
St. Paul, MN 55114
(800) 628-1337

Registers & Grilles
(grilles for screens)
453 West 17th Street
New York, NY 10011
(212) 243-7717

Summation Screens
(214) 321-2451

Troy
138 Greene Street
New York, NY 10012
(212) 941-4777

Seashells
Seashell Warehouse
1 Whitehead Street
Key West, FL 33040

Tiles
Nemo Tile
48 East 21st Street
New York, NY 10010
(212) 505-0009

Solar Antique Tiles
306 East 61st Street
New York, NY 10021
(212) 755-2403
www.solarantiquetiles.com

Wall Treatments
Chemetal
(metallic laminates)
39 O'Neill Street
Easthampton, MA 01027
(800) 807-7341
www.chmetal.com

The Decorators Supply Corporation
3610 South Morgan Street
Chicago, IL 60609
(312) 847-6300

Window Boxes
Windowbox
817 San Julian Street, Suite 406
Los Angeles, CA 90014
(213) 622-1999
www.windowbox.com

Web Sites
Anthropologie
www.anthropologie.com

Design Within Reach
www.dwr.com

www.homeportfolio.com

Smith + Noble
(800) 560-0027
www.smithandnoble.com

www.stylewiz.com

Target Stores
(888) 304-4000
www.target.com

Tavolo
(800) 700-7336
www.tavolo.com

Williams-Sonoma
www.williams-sonoma.com

Photo Credits

Breaking the Rules is dedicated
to my muses Ali, Caitlin, and Aunt M.

Acknowledgments

Many thanks to my most stylish friends and other rulebreakers who allowed me to invade their private spaces and share their style secrets. I am especially grateful to Yaffa Assouline, Prosper Assouline, Gayle Benderoff, Bill Blass, Mario Buatta, Alexandra Champalimaud, Maxine de la Falaise, Sybille Denfert-Rochereau, Robin Duke, Grace Fletcher, Bettina Gabetti, Deborah Geltman, John Hall, Constance Herndon, Marianne Irmler, Donna Karan, Calvin Klein, Katel Le Bourhis, Suzanne McDonough, Bette Midler, Len Morgan, Georgette Mosbacher, Stephen Motika, Josie Natori, Peter Nygard, Pierre Passebon, Ursula Poczewski, Barbara Richardson, Marcia Riklis, Cynthia Rowley, Isolde Sauer, Gerald Schmorn, Ivan Terestchenko, Benoit Tschieret, Angus Wilkie, and Andreas Zadora. Additionally, I wish to thank Candace Chabannes, Denyse Rinfret, and Jennifer Genco who helped bring life to this idea.

SIMON & SCHUSTER
Rockefeller Center
1230 Avenue of the Americas
New York, NY 10020

SIMON & SCHUSTER and colophon are registered
trademarks of Simon & Schuster, Inc.

Designed by Assouline

Manufactured in England

10 9 8 7 6 5 4 3 2 1

Library of Congress Cataloging-in-Publication Data
   Ferer, Christy.
   Breaking the rules: home style for the way we
live today / Christy Ferer with Risa Palazzo;
principal photography by Jean-François Jaussaud
and Joshua McHugh.
                    p.   cm.
   Includes bibliographical references.
   1. Interior decoration—United States—History—
20th century. I Palazzo, Risa. II. Title.
   NK2004.F47 2001
   747—dc21   00-069814

ISBN 0-684-86609-9

Page 2

Patriotism Hits the Wall
Large flags, spread wall to wall, can function

almost like wallpaper. And color choice abounds,

depending on what country you choose.